## The Net-Works

# Marketing Your Website

Learn how to attract visitors
to your site and keep them
coming back for more!

**Tim Ireland**

# NET-WORKS

PO BOX 200
Harrogate
HG1 2YR
England

www.net-works.co.uk
Email: sales@ net-works.co.uk
Fax: +44 (0) 1423 526035

Net.Works is an imprint of Take That Ltd

ISSN: 1-873668-87-2

**Trademarks:**
Trademarked names are used throughout this book. Rather than place a trademark symbol in every occurance of a trademark name, the names are being used only in an editorial fashion for the benefit of the trademark owner, with no intention to infringe the trademark.

Printed and bound in The United Kingdom.

**Disclaimer:**
The information in this publication is distributed on an "as is" basis, without warranty. While very effort has been made to ensure that this book is free from errors or omissions, neither the author, the publisher, or their respective employees and agents, shall have any liability to any person or entity with respect to any liability, loss or damage caused or alleged to have been caused directly or indirectly by advice or instructions contained in this book or by the computer hardware or software products described herein. **Readers are urged to seek prior expert advice before making decisions, or refraining from making decisions, based on information or advice contained in this book.**

TTL books are available at special quantity discounts to use as premiums and sales promotions. For more information, please contact the Director of Special Sales at the above address or contact your local bookshop.

# Contents

# Preface

This is the part of the book where I get to talk to you directly.

Hi,

I wrote this book to make the Internet a better place, not only for those who wish to publish and promote, but also those who wish to read and learn. The Internet presents an amazing opportunity to both parties, but only if mutual respect exists.

In it, you will learn how to market your business in the most effective way possible; by giving your customers exactly want they want. Many of the 'old' rules don't apply to New Media, but this one certainly does.

Good luck!

## Acknowledgements

My wife Kate gets top billing here for her faith, patience and undying efforts. My parents (who are acknowledged writers themselves) provided both the genetic material and inspiration necessary for this book to exist. Even my parents-in-law helped in too many ways to list here.

Professional thanks go to Jeremy and Stefan Kerner for respecting my ideas, ability and direction - and also to Sam Michel for running the most useful mailing list on the planet.

Finally, it must be noted that this book is the result of many hours, days, weeks and months of direct research. Special web sites were created to judge not only the usability of online tools and methods, but also the behaviour of the web users themselves. A special 'thank you' goes out to the 264,871 unwitting participants who singularly came to be entertained, but collectively have done so much more.

# Introduction

**Before we start, it's important that you understand the difference between 'advertising' and 'marketing'. Advertising is more about attracting interest, usually in a commercial manner. Marketing is an all-encompassing term that covers the entire relationship between the producer and the purchaser, from product conception through to issues such as branding, delivery and customer service.**

Most advertising-based approaches on the Internet not only cost you money, but are widely unappreciated by web users. However, just about all other online 'marketing' books that are currently available deal primarily with advertising issues such as banner advertising and direct mail models. One such book, despite acknowledging that that up to 60% of traffic to the average web site comes through search engines and directories, restricted information regarding this to a mere three pages.

This book is different. It acknowledges that even something as 'simple' as search engine success depends just as much on what you have to offer as how you list it. We'll be outlining why this is the case throughout the book, but for now you should at least be aware that even the most sophisticated keyword tricks will not help you if your site is a complete waste of time (the next site is only a click away, after all).

This may seem like a bitter pill to swallow, but some research and work in this area will gain you many more benefits in the long-term than any banner or Spam campaign.

Yes, we are going to teach you how to arrange, list and promote your site in the most effective way possible (and even show you a few tricks along the way), but these techniques go hand in hand with your site's usability.

By offering something of value to potential customers and listing it in the most effective way, you can not only achieve stronger traffic results, but also make web users more receptive to your business message.

If this were a book about marketing in the real world, it would almost definitely be consigned to the 'guerrilla marketing' section - but as we are about to show you, the web is very, very different

*Chapter 1*

# Why the Web is Different

**Even if you have a few years of 'real life' marketing experience under your belt, you have a lot to learn - and unlearn - before attempting to market a web site. This is because the web is a very different medium frsom those you may be used to, and your marketing strategy has to adapt accordingly if you want to enjoy any kind of success.**

For a start, though there are some rough parallels to traditional marketing methods on the web, they perform in very different ways. This is primarily due to the nature of the medium and how its users wish to benefit from it.

## *Junk Mail vs Spam*

We all get unsolicited mail, pamphlets and circulars in real life. It fills the letterbox, it falls out of just about every newspaper or magazine you buy, and there are even distributors who offer it to you in the street. While some may feel militant enough to put a 'No Junk Mail' sign on their letterbox - and even fewer are motivated enough to complain about it - for the most part we passively accept it as an inevitable part of life.

The typical reaction to an unsolicited email (Spam) is very, very, different. Firstly, most web users value their connection time highly (particularly those few who still pay timed charges). Getting a bunch of unwanted messages every time you download your email is especially galling when you're paying for the privilege.

Secondly, the web is considered by many to be a tool of information and empowerment - and just about any commercial message delivered to a user in this medium is derided as an 'insult to their intelligence'.

Thirdly, and probably most significantly, the old model of 'complain and it goes away' doesn't apply in this case. Some unscrupulous Spammers will include instructions on how to 'unsubscribe from their mailing list', but only use this response to confirm that your email address is a valid and current one. Even complaining to the server where the Spam seemed to originate from is often a waste of time, as it's either an account the Spammer is expecting to lose and doesn't care about, or it is a completely fictitious account provided by a system known as an 'anonymous remailer'. As a result, the answer for most is to delete and forget. Consequently, if you Spam, you are most likely going to be ignored.

If this isn't enough to discourage you, then you should also consider that there are many individuals who devote a lot of time to fighting this practice. These people publish web sites, provide anti-spam software and even run action groups calling for tougher laws. If you Spam, it is a fair bet that you will come to the attention of someone with the time, motivation and ability to seriously mess with your business - and who may even choose to invade aspects of your private life. There have been many instances of calls to a home number in the middle of the night, and worse, as a result of Spam.

## Television/Radio/Print Ads vs. Banners & Buttons

Banners and buttons are the Internet version of that traditional model where someone who has access to a large audience charges money for advertising time/space. Sadly, this technique just doesn't work for most businesses, but we're unlikely to see its demise anytime soon for a number of reasons.

Commercial messages are widely ignored on the Internet. So, unless a banner is particularly clever or entertaining, the best it can hope for is around a 1% click-through rate (i.e. only one out of every hundred people who see your 'ad' will click on it).

So why does this practice continue? Well, for a start, most of the people buying or selling such space come from a traditional marketing background, and this is an easy model for everybody to understand. Also, the figures are slightly better for large companies as there is some value in branding ('they don't have to click on it, they just have to see it') and they can afford to target such campaigns to a marginally more receptive audience. Of course, while big names continue to use this method, many smaller names will aspire to it, so the cycle carries on.

## Web Site vs. Brochure

Many companies can, and do, think of a web site as a brochure with unlimited pages that they can update instantly and distribute to millions of people. Sadly, the millions rarely turn up and most that do will never return. Why?

Well, those who surf the web are after something - usually information, entertainment or sex (though not necessarily in that order). If your site doesn't provide anything of value to them, they will feel somewhat offended and just go elsewhere for what they're seeking. Remember that they consider their time to be at a premium, and the next site is just a click away. Add to this the general intolerance of commercialism and you can see why taking a traditional approach to this new technology simply won't work.

And, as you may be beginning to suspect, there are few methods that are effective in driving people to a site in the first place. Your best bet is to provide what your target audience wants and let them find you.

## How do I Attract Visitors to My Site?

The key word here is 'attract'. As most traditional commercial models don't work, the best strategy you can employ to increase traffic to your web site is to make it worth coming to in the first place. Your potential customers are on the web looking for something, so you have to figure out what that is and provide it.

The following analogy may seem a bit fishy, but it's the best way to explain how this works.

There's a lake, well stocked with a variety of fish. Subject A is a seasoned fisherman who knows the kind of fish he wants to catch. He uses a rod, reel and a lure tailored to that specific fish. Subject B is a kid using a piece of string with a bent pin on the end who relies of a few juicy worms as his bait.

Subject C seems to have the advantage, as he has spent a lot of money on a boat that puts him right in the middle of the lake. He has no fishing equipment, but is quite confident that if he yells at the fish loud enough, they will be more than happy to jump into the boat with him.

- **Subject C**, of course, is unlikely to catch anything.

- **Subject B** may get a few nibbles, but it's unlikely he will be able to snare anything, and certainly has no guarantee of the type of fish he might catch.

- **Subject A** knows what he wants, and has planned for it. He not only knows what kind of bait to use, but also how to tug the line, plant the hook and reel in his catch.

## Advertising Bad - Information Good

It may be difficult to accept, but there are no 'quick-fix' options for marketing your web site and you should put such thoughts out of your mind immediately. Your best chance for success lies in knowing as much as possible about your target audience, carefully planning your web site to make it a resource they will be attracted to, then capturing your sales by placing product information adjacent to (or strategically within) this resource.

There are, however, quite a few measures you can take to make sure that your site is amongst the top results when your target audience goes looking for the information you provide. Most of this involves the intelligent use of the major search engines and directories.

A lot of your success will rely on knowing enough about how they work to list your site effectively.

## The Differences between Search Engines and Directories

**Search Engines** - are huge databases of the web sites that have been submitted to them. They rely heavily on automated systems both to catalogue the listings, and rank them when a user searches their database. The methods used to rank a site vary from engine to engine.

**Directories** - use 'people power' to catalogue and arrange web sites submitted to their database into categories. Each site submitted is viewed by a real person, who writes or amends the submitted page description and places it live in the appropriate category if they consider the site relevant and worthwhile.

**Hybrids** - a lot of the major search engines, in addition to their primary database, also have an edited directory of their own. Of course, sites that have been reviewed in such a section usually get listed first in any given set of search results. Getting listed in such a way used to involve more luck than skill, but this situation is changing as will soon be revealed.

Chapter 2

# About Search Engines

Your success with search engines will rely on knowing enough about how they work to list your site effectively. Search engines have three major automated functions:

- **Function One: The Submission**
  This is the initial submission of a single web page. The URL of the page is stored and scheduled for reading and/or 'crawling'.

- **Function Two: The Harvesting**
  The search engine 'visits' the submitted page and reads the material it considers relevant to their database (for some it is the written content, for others it is the hidden META Tags). During this visit, many search engines will go on to visit and read any connected pages within the site and catalogue them also. This is known as 'spidering' or 'crawling'.

- **Function Three: The Search**
  This is the main function of a search engine, where it responds to the query of the user and presents them with a list of matching results, ranked according to what it considers to be the most relevant. How this is done differs greatly from engine to engine.

## How Search Engines rank their Results
Some of the factors that search engines consider when ranking sites according to any search query include:

- **Page Title -**
  Preference is given if one or more of the keywords appear in the title of a page.

- **URL -**
  Similar to above, but focusing on the domain and/or document name that comprises the URL.

- **Keywords -**
  Rank is decided according to keyword relevance (also proximity if multiple words are used)

- **Description -**
  The 'description' META tag is scanned at this level for relevant keywords, but has more impact when someone searches for a particular phrase that you have used to describe the site.

- **Page Text -**
  The engine scans and stores the text (or a section of it) into its database. This method is usually used in preference to META tags, which are considered potentially misleading.

---

## What are META Tags?

META Tags are essential sections in the 'head' of a HTML document. Many search engines rely on these to let them know what the page is about. It's like a digital library card and is composed of three major parts:

- **Title** - the formal name of the page.
- **Description** - a short description of what the page is about
- **Keywords** - relevant words pertaining to the subject matter of your site

*Note - the 'Title' isn't formally a META Tag, but as it is held in the 'head' of the document along with the 'description' and 'keywords', and is often given equal or higher attention for ranking. It is just as important and should be grouped accordingly.*

---

- **Popularity -**
  Where a site/page is favoured because a number of other web pages (within their database) link to it. This often counts for even more if the link to it is on a page that is 'popular' in its own right.

- **Quality (Category Preference) -**
  If a web site is of sufficient quality to be listed in the category section of a 'hybrid' search engine, then those that have been reviewed in this section (and are relevant to the search) are often placed at the top of the results.

## How Alta Vista Works

- Page Title
- Keywords
- Description
- Page Text
- Category Preference

Alta Vista is the most sophisticated META Tag reader in that it is case sensitive - meaning that a search including 'UK' will give you a different result from 'Uk' or 'uk'.

This needs to be kept in mind when drafting the page description, and special attention needs to be paid to include both the capitalised and lower case versions of certain keywords (e.g. 'New York' and 'new york').

Alta Vista also 'reads' the full text of the submitted page and stores it in the database for ranking purposes. Placement is judged according to how high in the document the word appears, how often, and - if multiple search words are used - their proximity to each other within the document.

Sites featured in their category section are also placed highly, with the category information itself being drawn from The Open Directory Project.

# How Excite Works

- Page Title
- Page Text
- Category Preference

Excite primarily looks at the page title to rank results, so here a long and descriptive page title (with a maximum of 70 characters) is the best plan of action. Excite will also rate a page higher if the words used in the query are repeated in the page text (and in close proximity if multiple words are used).

If a site from their category section matches a search query, this will be presented at the top (along with a link to that category). The category section is edited by their own staff.

# How Google Works

- Page Text
- Popularity

Google primarily uses the words within any given web page to gauge its relevance. This might seem like a simple approach - but there's a lot more to it than might first appear.

Google ranks its results according to how many pages in its database link to it (how popular those pages are also affects this ranking). Subsequently success in Google relies not only on general link popularity from the masses, but also successful submissions to large category directories such as Yahoo!. A listing at the Open Directory Project also carries a lot of clout here.

Google also takes a look at the text surrounding the links on these other pages, as these words often describe the links that point to it. In this way they are indirectly using people power to improve the 'intelligence' of the search. This explains why Microsoft became the top result for searches like "guide to world domination" and "more evil than satan himself".

Finally, Google is not only a notorious 'crawler', but also stores the entire text content of submitted web sites in its database.

Subsequently a site with a lot of information or archived material casts a very wide net.

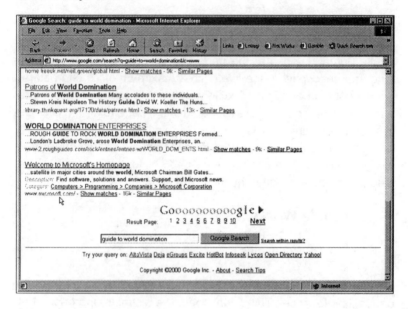

## *How Hotbot Works*

- Page Title
- URL
- Keywords
- Description
- Page Text
- Category Preference

HotBot is primarily META Tag reliant, so it really pays to get it right here. Ranking is decided on page title, then frequency/proximity of words in the keywords, description, and text respectively. HotBot also places high value on keywords appearing in the URL.

As with Alta Vista, some preference is given to sites featured in their category section, also drawn from The Open Directory Project.

# How Infoseek Works

- Title
- Keywords
- Description

Infoseek places its faith almost exclusively in the META Tags of any given page. As a result, it can index pages faster (often in 'real time') but details of the site are limited to the 200 characters allowed for the description and the 1000 characters permitted for keywords.

Here the secret is in maximising use of the keywords, taking care to include important word groupings (and keeping relevant words as close together as possible). For example, the following set of keywords would perform higher for 'white rose' than it would for 'red rose'.

```
<META NAME="Keywords" CONTENT="red white rose">
```

In this case, however, the ranking would be equally high for the same search.

```
<META NAME="Keywords" CONTENT="red rose, white rose">
```

This proximity rule also applies to the page title, and careful phrasing in the description is all-important. It should emulate, as closely as possible, what someone who is looking for the site might type when launching their search.

# How Lycos Works

- Page Title
- Keywords
- Description
- Page Text
- Popularity
- Category Preference

While Lycos does look at the META Tags, it looks more to the full text of any listed document when ranking the pages. Also, Lycos is highly 'punctuation intolerant' when it comes to header information, so punctuation should be avoided (especially in the page title) and META Tags should be kept short and simple. It also pays to repeat the core words in the opening text of the document, so they get read by Lycos before it trips over on that 'one full-stop too many'.

Again, those category listings get top billing - and yes, yet again, these come straight from the Open Directory Project.

## How Webcrawler Works

- Page Text

As the name would suggest, this Excite sister engine is primarily a crawler. Just like Excite, it ignores the header information and places more importance on word relevance, frequency and proximity within the actual document.

As with Google, the winners on Webcrawler are large sites with a lot of information. Most who find such a site through Webcrawler would be coming from a single article or product, and rarely through the 'front door' (index or entry page).

*Note -  While this information was correct at the time of going to print, you should be aware that some minor variations are likely over time.  To keep up with any changes you might want*

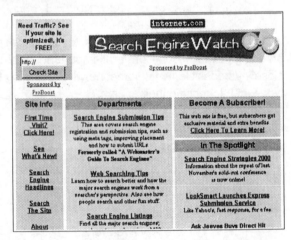

*to visit 'Search Engine Watch' at **www.searchenginewatch.com** for news on the latest developments.*

*Chapter 3*

# 'Tailored' Multiple Entry Pages

While the index page is generally recognised as the 'front door' of a site, you would be a fool not to open a side door or two to capture additional traffic. Some sites do this by producing multiple entry pages with special META Tags focused on each individual aspect of their site. In this way they hope to include more related words to that single subject in the keywords and descriptions and thus cast a wider net.

This really is looking at it from the wrong direction, as while you may be considered relevant in a wider variety of search queries, it won't do you much good unless you are ranked highly enough to benefit. The secret to getting the very top result lies in producing a targeted and unique resource - and then listing that resource with specific entry vehicles tailor-made for each search engine you wish to submit it to. (Of course, if you do have more than one resource that web users may consider valuable, it would pay to take this focused approach with each of them.)

As we said before, this resource is what the majority of web users will be looking for. By focusing your entry pages on the promotion of your resource and tailoring structurally to the unique ranking method of each search engine, you maximise your chances of making it into the top set of search results.

This technique lets you make the very most of the elements the search engine will be looking for, be it the page title, keywords, description, page text or other factors in the combination that it favours most. It also allows you to prioritise those vital keywords more effectively and gives you room to experiment with others (more on this in Chapter 10).

## Creating Effective Entry Pages

The creation of a truly effective entry page presents you with somewhat of a design challenge. As these pages first need to be easily read by the search engine 'robots', it's very important to keep graphics to a minimum and present the most relevant text to an expected search query right at the top of the document.

This is where it gets difficult, as such pages not only have to cater to the intricacies of the search engine's automated system, but also make a good first impression on those web users who find you via this doorway (see Chapter 8 on issues of trust). Additionally, you cannot automate the function that gets web users through to the main site (this will almost definitely foul up the search engine's automated system) so you have to make the links through to the main site as clear and as accessible as possible to guarantee a 'click through'.

One of the best ways to achieve both aims is by making multiple versions of the 'about us' page for this purpose (rather than trying to emulate the index page) and including links to the relevant section(s) you are describing in your text. This not only allows you to use a lot of descriptive text that will seem more than justified to the web user who finds you in this way, but also lets them to get straight to the area of the main site they are most interested in.

If you wish, you can include a major graphical link to the main site under this vital text. This should make clear what is information and what is navigation.

---

*Note - you must be careful to make sure that this major link is apparent without scrolling (i.e. immediately visible upon arrival).*

---

Remember, while linking to the main page (and/or other areas of the site) this link should not be reciprocal. These will just be doorways or portals by which the individual finds their way into the site through any particular search engine. Of course, you can make a generic 'about us' page available via the index page with much the same content, but linking to all five 'doorway' versions here would be silly.

Having links pointing to your specially tailored pages within your site can also get you blacklisted. A page that is specially designed to cater for the needs of one search engine may very well violate the rules of another. If the search engine is able to 'spider' to this page from another on your site, it could very well register an offence and automatically blacklist your domain. Such misunderstandings are very hard to clear up, so it's very important that your tailored pages link to other pages in the site, but that none link back.

All care should be taken to make sure that you submit the correct tailored page to the corresponding search engines.

## Your Tailored Entry Pages

### Entry Page 1 - Alta Vista
Alta Vista is the only META Tag reader that is case sensitive, so this entry page will be designed with headers to suit.

### Entry Page 2 - Excite
Excite is the only search engine to place high importance on the page title, so this page will have a long and descriptive title, taking full advantage of the 70 character maximum.

### Entry page 3 - HotBot
HotBot not only looks at the page title and META tags, but also the URL. So as well as the usual measures (page title, keywords & description) you can gain a few points here by naming the document itself something like 'importantkeyword.htm' rather than 'aboutus.htm'

### Entry Page 4 - Infoseek
Infoseek has a proximity rule regarding keywords in particular. These META Tags will need to be tailored accordingly.

**Entry Page 5 - Lycos**
No punctuation in the page title - especially ampersand (&), percent sign (%), equals sign (=), dollar sign ($) or question mark (?). Punctuation should also be minimised in the page text.

*Note - When naming your pages, try to make them as inconspicuous as possible. If a web user looks up at the address window and sees the file name of the page they are visiting is 'lycos_entry.htm' or even 'aboutus4.htm', they may feel that they have been tricked into coming to your page. (Of course this method is perfectly above board, but some web users are funny about being strategically targeted in any way.)*

*Of course, you will need to name the pages with different file names, but keep these as discreet as possible and above all make a very careful note of which file name relates to which search engine. Here is an example list of some 'discreet' file names matched to their corresponding targeted search engine.*

| | |
|---|---|
| *about.htm* | *Alta Vista* |
| *aboutus.htm* | *Excite* |
| *keyword.htm* | *HotBot* |
| *aboutsite.htm* | *Infoseek* |
| *about_site.htm* | *Lycos* |

*You can use any variation on this you wish, but remember that naming the page with an important keyword means a ratings boost in HotBot.*

## Don't Forget the Index Page
Index Page - Alta Vista, Lycos, HotBot, Infoseek, Lycos, Webcrawler, Google

The main index page should be registered separately with all of the major search engines - even those you have already submitted a tailored entry page to. Lycos, for example, has a 'popularity' feature much like Google's, and as the 'index' is the page most people would link to, you must submit this to take advantage of the ranking boost that it provides. It will also match the URL featured in the category section of any directories you may be listed with, meaning a further raise in ranking for this listing.

The index page (and the pages for each major section of your site) must have a combination comprising of as many of the key ranking elements that they can accommodate comfortably. While not all of these search engines read META Tags, most display elements from them and many will 'crawl' beyond the main page and catalogue anything found beyond, so you want these entries to be as accommodating and complete as is practically possible.

Later in this book, you'll discover ways to encourage web users to link to your site and thus improve your ranking, but first you need to focus on what will be your biggest ranking boost in a majority of search engines - successful directory listings.

*Chapter 4*

# About Directories

**Getting listed in a directory is a lot more straightforward and involves few technical considerations, as it mostly involves a human being looking at your site and listing/reviewing it accordingly. This however, presents its own complications.**

The primary consideration here is the quality of the site. As it is going to be viewed and judged by a real person it is very important not to attempt a submission until the site is fully functional.

The site is also judged on relevance, and the onus is on the publisher of the web site to choose which category (or sub category) the site belongs in. To do this, you have to go to the category that you consider to be most suitable, then click on the submissions/ suggestions link in that section. The details you submit are then sent to the editor(s) of that category. You provide these details via an online form that will usually ask for the URL, page title and a description. This is not the kind of thing you want to draft 'on the fly' for a number of reasons.

Directories only make use of the page title and description you provide for search ranking. They do not take META Tags or even page text into account - so important keywords and phrases have to be worked into the page title and description wherever possible. Sometimes a keyword in the URL can boost your rating, but unless it is in the domain name itself it doesn't pay to mess around here with a special entry page (like **www.domain.com/keyword.htm**). Because you are dealing with a human editor (who is not as easy to fool as a robot) creating such an obvious diversion is unlikely to impress. Rather than take the risk, it's usually best to stick with the original 'index' page for your URL submission and kiss this ranking factor goodbye.

This leaves you with the title and description - a challenge to say the least. You are not only limited to around 25 words for your description, but you have no guarantee that this, or indeed the title, will come through the editing process without alteration. You can minimise tinkering with your description by making it as objective as possible. But a lot of thought has to go into this process - balancing the need for keywords and a positive message with what you can really only guess the editor will let you get away with. A close look at the other sites in that category and how they fared can give some guidance here but, in the end, restraint and objectivity are the key.

Additionally, there are often significant delays in getting listed (up to 8 weeks in some cases) due to the human factor involved. This is especially frustrating when you consider there is no guarantee that you will even be listed, and you usually have no idea as the weeks drag by whether you are in a queue or have already been rejected. This makes judging when to re-submit the site very difficult.

There is one directory, however, that does not share this last problem. It is also the directory in which a single category listing can get you better results in many of the major 'hybrid' search engines, so it should be the first port of call in any submission strategy.

## How the Open Directory Project Works

Rather than rely on paid editorial staff, the ODP uses volunteers. Ordinary web users nominate a category they are interested/expert in, then register to become an editor. Because the submission and editing system is largely automated, just about anyone can use the system, and as a result the Open Directory Project has grown exponentially to rival - and some think conquer - Yahoo! itself.

At last count, Yahoo! had an estimated 1.2 million sites in its index and 150 staff editors. Early in 2000, the Open Directory Project had listed over 1.5 million web sites, organised into more than 200,000 categories by more than 22,000 volunteer editors.

Using the sheer power of numbers, (and a very efficient self-regulating system) the ODP can have you listed much faster than Yahoo!. In fact, most submissions are dealt with within 48 hours.

Also, because it lists submissions so efficiently, its database is far more up to date than Yahoo!'s and it is not only increasing in popularity in its own right, but also seeing its content farmed out to many of the big 'hybrid' engines to replace their own struggling category sections. Such listings, of course, rank much higher than others not listed in the category section.

AOL, Google, HotBot, Lycos and many others use ODP material, and in most cases the review you receive in the ODP will be repeated word for word, so while a successful listing here may seem easy, getting it right can often prove to be crucial.

## How Yahoo! Works

The main problem encountered by those submitting sites to directories such as Yahoo! are the delays resulting from a lack of editorial staff (submissions can take anything from 6 to 8 weeks to process at the best of times). As hard as they may try, it's very hard to keep up with the millions of web sites available with only a couple of hundred editors. In fact, it's widely reported that many submissions simply fall by the wayside due to overloading.

Add to this the general 'selective' nature of such a directory, and you may start to see why less than 30% of the sites submitted to Yahoo! actually get listed.

## How Ask Jeeves Works

Ask Jeeves is a very different model to other directories in that in is question-based. In fact if the submitted site does not provide a valid answer to one of their 10 million registered questions, you probably won't even get a look in.

As submissions are a simple notification of the URL by direct email, you have virtually no control over where or how it is placed. This is left ent- irely to the judgement of their editors, so the site really has to stand on its own.

Additionally, Ask Jeeves has one of the toughest editorial policies around and commercial sites especially are looked at with a very critical eye. Not only will they need to have all the polished qualities of a professional site (polished look, fast to load, easy to read and navigate) but they also need to be 'well-maintained, regularly updated and credible sources of information'.

Again, we come back to the quality of your page and what it has to offer. By now it should be clear why providing a useful resource is a top priority - regardless of what you have to sell.

Chapter 5

# Creating a Relevant and Unique Resource

'Content is king', as the Internet maxim goes, but not all material is valuable. There is a lot of talk at the moment about 'information pollution', as there are so many commercial pages that simply tout a service and even worse, so many more personal pages that seem to serve no purpose whatsoever.

Directories, (and to a lesser extent, search engines) do their best to filter the junk out, but avoiding it is almost impossible. For this reason, the average web user not only expects to see many examples of this, but is also conditioned to immediately recognise anything that is a potential waste of their time and simply look elsewhere.

## Choosing your 'Bait' Resource(s)

Creating a resource that is of value to potential customers not only increases your chances of getting found, it also displays a level of good-will to those who find you. This not only greatly improves your chances of securing a 'sale', but also makes the Internet a slightly better place to be.

But, with over a billion web pages available on the Internet, some research and creativity is required on your part to make sure that the information you are providing is:

- Something of value
- Relevant to your business
- Likely to be sought by your customers
- Reasonably unique

You may have offered something of value to attract customers in the past. A 20% discount, say, for those who 'mention this ad/brochure'. While this may have an impact on closure (and is certainly relevant to your business), it is not something that the typical web user will be searching for and by no means unique. Most of those using the Internet are on the lookout for:

- Information
- Entertainment
- Freebies
- Sex

## Information

Despite what you may have read, it is information that typical web users spend most of their time looking for. It is also the easiest and safest option for most small businesses to present on the web.

If you capture someone in your target market whilst they are looking for hard information, it is more likely that they will be in a mood to do business when they happen across your site. Additionally, if you provide them with something of value upon arrival, their choice of who to do business with will swing in your favour considerably.

**But what kind of information should you provide?**
Something close to the ideal web model would be a brochure offering 'advice for the potential homeowner', published by a bank or loan provider. The advice given in such a case can only be seen as impartial if it deals with matters not directly linked to the choice of mortgage. Likewise, if you plan on providing advice to your customers, it should empower them in a way that is closely linked to your business, but does not directly involve what you have to offer.

A good example here would be a real estate agent providing information about the local shops and facilities. A web user looking to move into a new area is more than likely to research it on the Internet first, and a related business such as this can benefit greatly from providing such targeted information. An added touch could include a few handy numbers that will help those moving into a new home get the phone connected, the electricity running and a pizza delivered to their door once all of the boxes are unloaded. This is both helpful, closely related to the nature of the business and - due to the specific nature of the information - more likely to be unique.

If advice is what you primarily deal in (i.e. if you're an educational publisher, lawyer, consultant etc.) then the best strategy is to offer a sample of your wares. An extract from your book or a sample report will not only enable the web user - but also put your skills on show. Even an author of fiction can benefit from the 'information' model by publishing the research that went into the book.

---

*Note - A commercial site that is 'information based' is more likely to get listed favourably in the directories.*

---

### Entertainment

The entertainment/humour option should be approached with great caution. Firstly, a lot of talent is involved in creating something truly entertaining. You would have to cast a very careful eye over your own ability (or that of your web author) before you took this step. Secondly, one minor error in judgement here could alienate potential customers and/or reflect badly on your professional image.

On the plus side, the Internet community is a quirky one to say the least, so a new slant on an otherwise saturated topic is not only likely to give you the 'uniqueness' you require, but also strike a chord with a wide audience. But remember that it is the targeted audience that you are most likely to benefit from. Will your potential customers be looking for such a site in the first place?

The public action site at **www.urban75.com** gets thousands of visitors a week to their highly entertaining (and satisfying) 'punch gallery'. This allows web users to take an online swipe at the likes of Bill Gates and Rupert Murdoch - and is so popular that it also receives wide coverage in mainstream media.

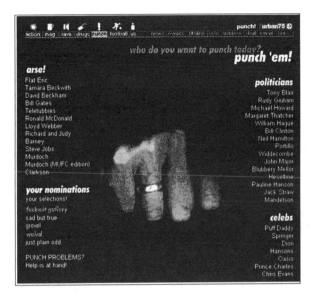

## Freebies

The word 'free' is probably one of the most overused and misleading words on the Internet, but used in conjunction with your specific business it can attract a potential customer on the lookout for a bargain.

The offer should be substantial (i.e. not a 'free quote') and closely tied to a further relationship with your company. Downloadable free software or 'shareware' is an excellent example of this model and quite prevalent on the web. The user gets a usable product absolutely free of charge, and if suitably impressed will be back for more and/or willing to pay for the 'full' version of the program.

You can also use freebies to improve your data-capture. If the web-user wants a free widget mailed to them, they will find it more than reasonable if you ask them to fill in an online form with their address details. All that remains is for you to follow up the lead.

Competitions are another good example, whereby you offer visitors to your site a chance at one big freebie. There are also many sites that promote online competitions, so listing with the most popular of these can result in a great deal more traffic to your site.

The very popular site at **www.loquax.co.uk** offers web users links to the very latest online competitions in the United Kingdom. Listing your competition with such a site can result in a lot of extra traffic.

## Sex

Sorry, this is a book about the Internet and - like it or not - sex cannot be avoided. As with entertainment, great caution should be employed here for fear of alienating potential customers - but there is a way to employ sex to attract visitors to an otherwise 'straight' site. Humour.

Regular web users will be familiar with the usual tricks porn merchants get up to while trying to drive traffic to their pages. The most annoying of these is producing pages with reams of unrelated text in the hope that they will turn up somewhere among the results of a perfectly innocent search. Quite a few web authors have been turning this method on its head with some quite impressive results.

The highly ranked site **www.furnitureporn.com** (offering graphic pictures of chairs in compromising positions) regularly turns up in the top results of searches for 'furniture', primarily due to the large number of individuals who link to it and the many favourable listings it gets in the 'Humour' sections of directories. However, the author of this page has missed the point somewhat by trying to benefit from the traffic with a number of largely unrelated 'affiliate' schemes. If he actually sold furniture (or even just set up affiliated links to furniture providers) he could make a mint.

## *Finding Your Niche*

You should be aware that, with over a billion web pages available on the Internet, being unique is a top priority - and your greatest challenge. It doesn't matter if there are a few similar examples, so long as yours is better (and listed more effectively) you will prevail. However, if there are hundreds of thousands of pages like yours, achieving the magic 'top ten' result becomes almost impossible.

Also, while it pays to create a resource that potential customers might need or enjoy, you must also be careful to make it relevant to your products or services for it to have maximum effect. You also need to provide that little bit extra for those that eventually do business with you.

## *Customer Resources*

Any of the above methods can attract new visitors to your site, but even if you choose Entertainment, Freebies or Sex to attract visitors to your site, you will still need to provide 'information rich' sections for your potential, and existing, customers.

The Internet is an immediate and versatile tool that allows you to cater to this often forgotten half of marketing - customer care.

### Communicate With Your Customers

Your web site should allow your customers to contact you quickly and easily with any concerns or questions that they may have. To avoid getting a thousand emails a day with the same question, you can suggest web users refer to your series of 'FAQs' (Frequently Asked Questions) before they make an enquiry, but the customer should feel that they may contact you at any time with anything they might need.

### Inform Your Customers

An 'FAQ' is part of this, but shouldn't be the end. Think about all of the information that you can't fit in, or on, your current packaging that would be useful to the customer. A web site allows you almost unlimited space to include helpful material such as detailed product information, instructions, educational material and even ideas for product use. This not only displays goodwill to the customer, but also encourages use of your product(s). You can also use your web site to start an online mailing list, letting you alert your customers to new products, changes to your service, or special offers (more on this in Chapter 17).

Driving existing customers to such a site has many benefits, not the least of which being the potential reduction in wasted staff hours fielding the same questions day after day. Also, being informed and happy users of your products and services, existing customers can be one of your strongest proponents on the web, where 'word of mouth' rules supreme.

Taking visible steps to keep your customers in touch and informed can also have an impact on potential customers who visit the site. Those that see this high level of support will feel that much more comfortable about doing business with you. It also allows you to provide a strong sales message in a world where hype is abhorred.

## Information Rich, Copy Light

While it pays to have an 'information rich' site, the message that is meant to convert users of your site to your products or services should be short, objective, and to the point (see previous chapter). This is where a lot of sites fail as, while it pays to use this 'unlimited' space to empower potential and existing customers, you should not use it to waffle on endlessly about how fantastic your company is.

If a web user is after a particular piece of information, then they will scan across entries and texts for keywords and links that are most relevant to their search, and move from page to page and site to site until they find what they want. It is only then that they will be likely to read the information in full (usually after printing it out).

Keeping this in mind, most web users who find their way to your resource(s) will have completed one of these journeys. Those that stick around may very well decide that the next thing they want is one of your products. Their journey to securing this product needs to be as easy and straightforward as possible. As such, your sales message should be short, to the point, and lead straight to a facility that lets them secure your products and/or services. The location of the 'store' within your site should also be obvious and, once they get there, easy to use. Chances are that they've already made their decision; so let them get on with it!

## Weaving with Hyperlinks

Remembering what we said about scanning, the average web user's eye can be caught using bold or coloured text, but if you really want them to 'follow' what you are saying, you need to use a Hyperlink.

The more relevant the 'bait' resource is to your business, the easier it is to weave your sales message in with hyperlinks to your products. Put simply, whenever you mention one of your products by name, you put a link to the page where more details about that product appear. If from this page they are able to purchase the product immediately, then all the better.

## Your Resource as a Sales Tool

This would be the most obvious method for those offering an online sample of their wares, such as an extract from a book or 'free' software, as you are not only providing something of value but also a sample of the product or service in question.

Make the sample you provide as useful as possible, but make sure that you let the customer know in as subtle a way as possible that more is available should they want it. For example, the 'free' software would have a lot of features and functions that, while disabled in the 'free' version, still appear in menu choices. Ideally, an option within the software would allow them to register, pay online and use these extra functions within minutes. This is a model widely used by software distributors.

## Testimonials as a Sales Tool

The people visiting your site have never met you or seen your offices and, unless they are aware of your branding, have no reason to trust you other than by what they see on your web site. Testimonials can go a long way to gaining the trust of a 'new' customer, and can also introduce a very strong sales message.

Don't mess around with this. Web users are very canny, and can smell a fake or otherwise insincere testimonial a mile away. The best way to ratify your testimonials is to include the name of the referee and a 'mailto' hyperlink within that text so the new visitor can check up on this opinion if they wish. Virtually no one will do this of course, but the fact it is there will add considerable strength to the words. (Of course, if you take this measure, you will need the permission of the referee involved.)

The testimonials should also, like your sales copy, be short and to the point. You want visitors who see these to be able to take them in at a glance, so it may even pay to highlight the most relevant word(s). Of course, while we're on the subject of highlighting, if the testimonial mentions a product of yours by name it would be foolish not to include a hyperlink to that product within the text.

*Chapter 6*

# How to Hold Your Audience
## (And Keep Them Coming Back)

**Before you draft your written content, you should be aware of a few things regarding the medium and the habits of web users themselves. For a start, nearly all of the visitors to your site will be reading from a computer screen. This alone slows reading time by about 25%, and after a while can really start to strain the eyes (especially if the web site is poorly designed and the text is difficult to read).**

You should also be aware that web users have a notoriously short attention span, and are unlikely to want to wade through mountains of text to find what they want - especially when another site is only a click or two away. Add to this the value many web users place on their surfing time (particularly those on a connection who pay by the minute) and you actually run the risk of insulting them if you don't get to the point quickly and succinctly.

Research has also shown that web users scan rather than read even the briefest of web documents, picking out words, sentences or paragraphs that interest them. When doing this they will invariably keep an eye out for any large, bold or especially linked text to get them where they want to be just that little bit faster.

Linked text (text that includes a 'hyperlink' allowing the user jump to another page or site with a click) stands out in particular, not only because it is a different colour and underlined, but also because it is instantly recognisable by web users as the source of more information.

However, it is important to use restraint when inserting links, as having too many makes them harder to scan and therefore pointless. Be warned that this does not mean you should break up a large amount of text and link it page by page. Breaking up your information in an effort to make it seem shorter just makes it harder to read all in one go, and almost impossible to print.

So make it short. Really short. In fact, take what you would normally write for a printed version of your document and cut it by half - if not more. Also, be aware that most visitors are only going to give your text a brief overview. You should not try to force them to read the whole thing, as many will simply give up and go elsewhere. Instead, you should play to your audience by making your pages easier to scan and linked to relevant information where relevant or necessary.

As you can see, we've waffled on for several paragraphs before getting to the point - and this would never do on a web site. Instead, the above information would be delivered in the following format, with the main point(s) being delivered immediately (if not within the header or title itself).

---

## Writing Effective Web Copy

- **Keep it Short**
Write at least 50% less text than you would normally use.

- **Make it Easy to Scan**
Make key points easy to see by using strong headers and bold text (not Italics, which are hard to read on screen).

- **Use Links**
Use a hyperlink when you mention another page or site that may be of use to the reader.

- **Make it Easy to Print**
Don't break up a topic to make it seem shorter - this only makes it harder to read and print.

---

The above text is not only less than a quarter the length of our opening paragraphs, but also covers the main points quickly, simply and in order of their importance. Were more information to be required, the header could link to another page that covered the topic in more depth. In this way, you provide those who are interested in the information with easy access to it, but avoid confronting them with a mass of text immediately upon arrival.

Nothing annoys web users more than having to 'scroll' on a main or index page. They should be able to see everything on offer at a glance so they can get where they want to be quickly and easily.

This applies also to your chosen resource page(s), but does not mean that you should skimp on the content here. Of course, you should make the introductory page to your resource(s) as brief and as clear as possible, making what is on offer easy to find and understand. But if it is information that you are providing as your resource, then the information itself should be as comprehensive as possible.

It should also be 'print friendly' as once the average web user hits the 'mother lode', they nearly always print it out. They do this mainly because large amounts of text are hard to read on screen, but they also want to make sure that they have a copy of the information that they can keep. Don't be offended, but sites do come and go, and they cannot be sure that the information will still be there when they return.

## About 'Sticky' Content

Providing 'sticky' content, is not only a matter of constantly referring and linking to other areas or products within your site (see next chapter on 'Weaving with Hyperlinks') but having all of the related tools and information that a visitor might need immediately to hand.

This means that if further reading might be beneficial with regards to your products or resource, then this information should be available on your site. If the information requires a glossary, then there should be a glossary available on your site. If your resource requires a specific need such as monetary conversion, then there should be a tool to do this on your site.

The last thing you want to do is give the visitor cause to go to another site, as you may very well lose them. However, the concept of 'sticky' content needs to be balanced with credibility. If you can provide links to external sites that back up what you have to say or include short testimonials from customers/visitors complete with links to their email address, this will boost your credibility a great deal. Some elements of your marketing strategy may also involve the creation of one or two pages specifically for linking to other sites.

Such links can be included without sacrificing your 'stickiness', simply by configuring them to spawn a new window. This is quite a simple code technique that is widely used to make the 'new' web site open up in a separate browser window, thus keeping your page 'live' and helping to ensure that the visitor returns.

The 'sticky' concept also requires that you to motivate the visitor to bookmark your site and/or return at a later date.

## *Keeping Their Interest, Updating Your Content*

Once a visitor has been to your site, what cause have you given them for coming back? Even if you update the information weekly or monthly, do they know that you do this?

You should make sure that web users who find your site know how often it is updated, and why such updates are valuable enough for them to return. The more they return, the more they are exposed to your sales message. They may not be in the mood to buy to today, but tomorrow could be very different.

You also need to give those who do become customers good cause to return by providing content that is of value to those who have invested in your products or services (see next chapter).

Both potential and existing customers can also be actively prompted to return to your site by the judicious use of mailing lists (see Chapter 17).

*Chapter 7*

# Turning Traffic into Sales

**Remember that the key to directory success (and subsequent search engine success) is the strength of your chosen resource(s) and a low-key 'sell'. If your web site screams of commercial interest, you may very well see the strength of your resources being overlooked.**

The key here is to show what you have on offer, and keep the sales message(s) subtle. This may go against the grain for some, but there are ways and means of maximising your sales message without the hype.

## *Customer Care as a Sales Message*

One easy way to weave-in an effective sales message is to have two separate sections for 'visitors' and 'customers'. Of course your 'bait' resource(s) will be in the visitors section, but if you found a site that offered a free and valuable resource to all and sundry, wouldn't you be the least bit curious as to the extra material that is available to customers?

This model works very well for those who have a wide product range. By including detailed product information and ideas/ instructions on how to use the product, you are not only providing a valuable resource for those who already buy them, but also helping to sell them to those who otherwise might not have considered the value of such a product.

Most of your potential customers on the web will be of the type that likes to think for themselves. By providing useful material about your product(s) you are catering to their need to come to an educated and 'independent' decision.

This way, just by lightly peppering your site with a few choice testimonials, you are not only swinging them closer to their 'independent' decision, but also showing them the way to a product or two.

## Making the 'Store' Separate

While the section that gives your formal sales message and/or allows web users to buy your products should be very easy to find (and use), it should appear at first glance to be a very separate section of the site, and by no means the main one.

Keep those resources as pure as possible (with the occasional subtle sales link of course) and you will gain the trust of those who come to your web site. Without this trust, you are not going to sell a thing.

*Chapter 8*

# Building It Right

**A large part of trust is confidence. You may remember a classic 'trust-building' exercise that involves you falling backwards and being caught by the person behind you. But what if the person chosen to catch you looks particularly weak? What if you saw them fall down a set of stairs, drop an entire tray of hot drinks and break three plates, all during one morning coffee break?**

While you may very well trust the intentions of that person to catch you, you may not have sufficient confidence in their ability to do so.

Your web site is, in effect, another shop front for your business. For many, it will be the only point of contact with your business before a possible decision to buy. If it does not instil confidence in the web user, then you are unlikely to make that sale.

You may know all there is to know about family law or nuclear fission, but if you cannot translate this knowledge effectively onto the web then you will have failed to communicate with your audience, and they simply will not listen to what you have to say.

This may seem unfair, but look at it from the web user's point of view. The Net is a channel of communication seen by them to be on par or superior to print, radio or television. A business with a ramshackle site gives the impression that they have not researched the medium thoroughly, or have so little respect for it that they are willing just to 'throw a site together' to get it out of the way.

> ## Hint
>
> *The Net-Works Guide to Creating a Website* has all the information a budding webmaster needs to plan and build a professional web presence, without the need to learn HTML.

You may be starting from scratch, or already have a web site and wonder why it isn't working. Either way, you need to take a close look at the structure of your site with an eye to improving its functionality and marketability.

## *Building It Yourself*

You don't have to be a seasoned webmaster to build a professional and effective web presence, but you do need to know what your limitations are.

If you try to do more than you are capable of, and the site fails with numerous 'bugs', then it is only the 'bugs' that users will notice. In the end you will look incompetent - definitely not a good thing. This goes especially for any site wishing to sell their goods online. Would you trust a 'real life' store with your credit card if the place were a complete mess with shelves falling off the wall?

Stealing the format or design of another web site may seem like a handy shortcut, but only makes you look like an incompetent thief. Most web users see hundreds, if not thousands of sites every week. They will recognise common themes, ideas and graphics, and may not onlsy reject your sales message outright on the basis of this, but also report you to the rightful owner for breach of copyright.

Even if you source such things legally, adding unnecessary graphics, bells and whistles to compensate for a lack of content or planning will only increase the time it takes for the page to load and make it look like more of a dogs dinner than it already is.

If you create a simple, yet useful and well-organised site, then the end result will be respected for its merits.

## *Hiring a Web Designer/Author*

As easy as building a web site can be, you may not be confident enough in your skills to build exactly what you want. Also, you may take a close look at the time it would take you to build and maintain a web site and decide that you may as well hire someone to do it. Fair enough. Your time is worth money, too.

While hiring a web design company may be beyond your budget, hiring a freelance web designer can often produce equal, if not better results, for much less money. Research, however, is vital here.

Seemingly, the most obvious thing to do here would be to look up 'web designer' on the Internet. Good luck. There are millions of them out there, and they range from serious webmasters to overconfident school-kids operating out of a shed in the back yard. Even when choosing from the more competent web designers, you will have to be careful to choose one that has the skills you need. One that specialises in graphics or special effects, for instance, may not have the slightest idea about secure e-commerce. Make sure you go looking for the skills you need.

Before you even contact a web designer, have a close look at their own site and those they have built for other businesses. Contact these businesses yourself, and ask what they thought of the service. Did they get value for money, was the project delivered as promised and to deadline?

Once you do make contact with a web designer, it is important to agree on what it is you want to achieve, what you want them to do to help you achieve it, and what it is going to cost.

Having read a book like this, you may even want to include a design brief showing your needs from a marketing point of view. This could include anything from your decisions on page titles and how the sections should be organised or presented, to writing your own copy and drafting your own META Tags for the web designer to insert into any necessary pages. Intelligent web designers will be happy to work with you on this, and listen to your needs.

Along the way, a lot of the smaller operators will offer 'domain name and hosting' or 'search engine submission' deals that aren't always the best value for money. Kind of like a bank that offers insurance and loans, when all you really want is someone to look after your money. Unless you're a complete novice, it often pays to search around and do a lot of this yourself. After all, you're hiring this person for their web design skills, so why stray from that?

Once you have your quote, shop around. Don't settle on the first offer you come across.

## *Hiring a Web Design Company*

If you want more than design only, then you need to move up to an organisation with the buying power and experience to achieve a total solution - but even here you must be careful.

As with a web designer, check out the company's site and those of their clients. By all means get a quote on your complete solution, but make sure it is a detailed one. For instance, if domain name and hosting is included in the quote, check the cost of this and do a bit of shopping around. If the cost they have quoted seems unfairly high, ask them about it.

As with an independent web designer, a web design company should be approachable about your marketing ideas and concerns. Do not assume that just because they can build a fantastic site that they know how to promote it. Ask about this side of the service and offer your thoughts on what should happen. If web site promotion isn't part of their usual remit, then offer them the elements that you wish to go into your site and take on the promotion yourself.

---

*Note - Whether you use a web designer or web design company, there is the issue of site access to be considered. While some site access is necessary to test such things as secure shopping areas, you need to ask yourself if you trust this individual or organisation to have ongoing access to your site.*

---

## *A Quick Note on Frames*

Frames break up the information shown in the browser window into two or more separate web pages, each independent of the other. Mostly this is used to present a 'constant' navigation bar that lets you choose other pages within the site. These are then displayed in the second (larger) frame.

In theory this makes it easier to organise larger sites, but in practice frames mean trouble. They make web pages harder to print, they make it very difficult to 'bookmark' a specific page within a site, and they can even stop your page from loading properly in some browsers. Funnily enough most web users hate them, but this isn't the only reason most commercial sites are now avoiding the use of frames.

Frames are deadly to any search engine strategy, as most harvesting robots will not be able to see past the first 'frame' of your navigation bar. If by some miracle the search engine manages to spider beyond and list the pages within your site, then those that find one of these pages through the search engine will more than likely load that single page only (i.e. they will not see the navigation bar).

Frames are a design and marketing headache, avoid them at all costs.

*Chapter 9*

# Domain Names

**If you're a very small company and you wish to host your web site on the free space offered to you by your Internet Service Provider, (your URL in this case would be something along the lines of http://www.ispname.com/businessname/) then go for it. A domain name isn't the be all and end all of your web presence, and many quality business sites have enjoyed success without one.**

That said, a domain name (especially a dot-com) is seen as a powerful branding tool that not only enhances customer confidence, but also makes you easier to find in a number of ways.

If you are serious about marketing your web site, then you will have to seriously consider what your domain name is going to be and how it is going to benefit you. You also need to make sure that it is bought sensibly and hosted correctly for it to be truly effective.

In short, a domain name is not necessary. Getting the right domain name and hosting solution is.

## *Why a Domain Name?*

### *Confidence*
A web site that is hosted at a short and snappy domain name gives the visitor to the web site your assurance that you are serious about the web - and here to stay.

### *Branding*
A good domain name can enforce the name of your product/ business or even have something strong to say about what it offers. It also makes promoting your web site in real life that

much easier (i.e. by including a memorable domain name on your letterheads, business cards, company vehicles etc. you strengthen your branding and make it easier for others to find your web site).

### Search Engines

Not only do some search engines give an added boost to a site that has a keyword in the domain name, but if in the future you decided to change where you host the site, you can do so without all of your search engine promotion going down the drain. This is particularly important if you plan on encouraging others to link to your site (see Chapter 14).

### Stability

A lot of companies fight to keep the same phone number, no matter the cost, as there are thousands of business cards and brochures floating around out there with this number on it. A good domain name has equal value. No matter what happens with your server or hosting, those looking for your site via your domain name or a link to it will find their way there for as long as you choose to keep it active.

## Why dot-com? (and 'Why Not?')

While officially being the domain suffix for the United States, '.com' is widely seen to be international, and the Park Avenue of web addresses. This makes things kind of tough if the domain name using your brand or company name is already taken (and with .com, you can bet this is the case). But it is worth the effort to try and secure an effective '.com' first, before investigating a local suffix (like .com.au, or .co.uk). The truly thorough will secure both.

It should also be noted that if your business is based primarily in one country, then sticking with a local domain only is perfectly acceptable. It may even benefit you in the end, as a lot of the localised search engines give ranking preference to sites using local domains.

## Why Hosting is Important

Many of the 'cheap' domain deals involve redirection, 'masked' or 'branded' hosting. This can not only look very shoddy to those who know how such things work, but also make it almost impossible for the search engine robots to list you properly. The methods these companies use differ greatly, so there is little point trying to cover all of the techniques here, but rest assured that just about all of these 'cheap' procedures will make you as good as invisible to the search engines.

If you are going to the expense of buying a domain name, then you have to make sure that the company who provides your web space will allow you to assign a domain name to that space.

For instance, you will almost certainly find that your ISP will not let you do this on your 'free' web space. For this reason, most businesses end up using a reputable 'virtual' host. Some of these hosts even offer pretty good domain name deals and email redirection as part of the offer, so shop around first.

---

*Note -*
*Even the 'free' space that your ISP provides can present problems. Some, like VirginNet for example, offer you a 'masking' option that lets you direct web users to an address like 'business.virgin.net/~yourname' when the actual assigned name is 'freespace.virgin.net/~yourname'. This may seem like a good measure to make your hosting choice seem a little more professional, but if you try to register the 'masked' address with a search engine it will not be able to see beyond it to your real page. Subsequently, you are forced to submit the 'freespace' address to the search engines if you wish to get listed at all.*

---

## Domain Name Dangers

Before you choose and secure a domain name, there are a couple of points that you need to consider.

## Copyright

As already noted, '.com' officially denotes a US site, so even if it is perfectly legal for you to use a chosen name in the United Kingdom, Australia or elsewhere, you may end up infringing a trademark or copyright that is held in the US if you wish to use the name at a dot-com address. Enforcement in this area is still in its infancy, but it's a headache you can well do without.

## Privacy

When you secure a dot-com domain name, the details under which you have purchased it are readily available to anyone who wishes to look them via a 'whois' search. For this reason, it always pays to use your business address and details when purchasing your domain name. Do you really want someone calling you at home with a question about your web site?

## Dot-Com Denial

Even if you have what you think is a reasonably unique brand or company name, chances are the dot-com for that name is already taken. Often this involves someone in the United States who also has a legitimate claim to it. Occasionally, however, you may find that 'your' name has been secured by a 'cybersquatter'.

A cybersquatter is also known as a 'domain name speculator' (and a few other names that can not be printed here). These entrepreneurs buy up domain names that they think will represent value to someone in the future, hoping to sell them at a greatly increased price.

*Tip*

If you believe your brand, trademark or other rights have been infringed then you should refer to the Internet Corporation for Assigned Names and Numbers at www.icann.org for more information.

If a cybersquatter has infringed your trademark or other rights, you may or may not have recourse to secure what is rightfully yours - but remember, enforcement in this area is still in its infancy. You may also find that, even if it is a registered trademark in your country, the dot-com is still officially a US domain, so only trademarks held in the United States are likely to carry any legal weight.

A lot of people refuse to do business with cybersquatters on principle, but, if the price they have set seems fair and reasonable, you may choose to settle things in the most straightforward manner and simply pay them. Alternatively, you can secure the name with a local domain. Here your trademark rights are stronger and your brand or company name is more likely to be available.

You may even choose to forgo branding in the domain name and instead use it as a powerful keyword tool, or use a combination of both.

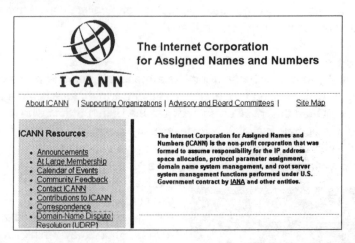

## *Choosing a Domain Name*

Your best bet in the overcrowded domain name market is using a combination of words, and possibly the careful and judicious use of a dash ('-'). This could involve teaming your brand or company name with a powerful keyword, or using multiple keywords to comprise a sales message or mission statement in your domain name.

When drafting ideas for your domain name, you should ask yourself the following questions:

- Is it easy to spell?
- Is it easy to remember?
- Does it look good in lowercase?
- Do the words naturally separate?

By 'natural separation', we mean the landscape of the words that, when presented running together, may or may not make clear where the first word ends and the next word begins. Rememberthatdomain-namesdonotallowforspaces (this is what the dash is for). Sometimes you will need to include a dash to define two separate words, and sometimes high and low letters will do it for you.

- 'High' letters: b, d, f, h, k, l, t
- 'Low' letters: g, j, p, q, y

The first example below seems to run together between the 'l' and the 'i' - 'lint' even seems to leap out at you from the middle of the name, thanks to it being a recognisable word in itself, and bounded by two 'high' letters that set it apart. Here a dash is necessary to separate the words and make the domain name that much more recognisable - and memorable.

**financialinternet.com**
**financial-internet.com**

In this example, the dash is necessary to define the branding for 'Net Works' and set it apart from the common computer term 'net-work'. It also looks fairly balanced thanks to the relatively evenly spaced 'high' letters in the domain name and the local domain suffix.

**net-works.co.uk**

Here no dashes are necessary, as the words in this straight-forward sales message are clearly defined and separated by 'high' and 'low' letters. This is also fairly well balanced in combination with the '.co.uk'.

**buymybook.co.uk**

These are more than simple aesthetic concerns (though you will want your domain name to look pleasing if you plan on using it on letterheads and brochures). Making sure that your domain name is instantly decipherable and memorable will strengthen your brand and aid retention for all those who see it.

## Looking up a Domain Name

Once you've got a few ideas sketched out, you are going to have to go to a domain name 'lookup' page (also known as a 'WhoIs' lookup) to find out which of your preferred combinations are available.

There are thousands of such pages and services, nearly all of which will confirm the availability of any name with the message 'buy it now' (a perfect example of providing a resource and turning it into a sale). Below we'll be recommending some of the better 'lookup' services on the Internet, but you should be aware that a better deal is nearly always out there. Sadly, taking the time to shop around could lead to heartache, as what was available yesterday could very well be taken tomorrow.

There have also been whispers of companies that run 'WhoIs' lookups taking choice domain names queried through their site for themselves. While a case has yet to be substantiated here, there certainly is enough smoke to cause alarm. Even if the domain name you query one day is gone the next purely by chance, it is very frustrating to go through this, so it is usually best to:

1. Research and settle on a good domain (and hosting/ assigning) deal first
2. Have a way of paying ready at your finger tips
3. Start with a strong 'wish list' of names and words
4. Use a reputable 'WhoIs' lookup that best suits your needs
5. Find the best available combination possible through this facility
6. Secure the available name you want immediately through your chosen registrar/vendor

# 'Whois' Lookups

## BetterWhois.com
### www.betterwhois.com

Now the domain business has been deregulated, many different domain registrars are granting domain names. Sometimes names come up as being 'available' when someone has actually already bought it (and the 'sale' has yet to register in the database you are searching). This special search engine lets you search all of the relevant databases for the major domains to find out who owns it.

## Allwhois.com
### http://allwhois.com

Here you can not only check the basic availability of your chosen domain name in .com, .net and .org, but also jump straight to the nation of your choice to check its availability for your local area.

## Domain Name Wizard
### http://rwm.net/virtualis/domainwizard

Rather than only letting you try one name or domain at a time, this site offers a few creative solutions by providing a selection of variations based on your business name (and a few keywords if you so choose).

## Domainator
### http://www.e-gineer.com/domainator/

This great service checks whether your planned domain name is already taken, violates a US trademark, or might have an alternate meaning in a foreign language (those who bought a Mitsubishi 'Pajero' will be aware of the dangers here). It even searches for rhymes and suggests combinations of multiple words if you wish.

*Chapter 10*

# Keywords: What are They Looking For?

Once you've built a resource that potential customers will want to find, you need to make sure that you are found easily. A lot of your success in the search engines will hinge on how accurately you judge what those looking for you will type as their search query.

These words and phrases will be the building blocks of your page titles, META Tags and even page text. In some cases, you may even choose to include important keywords in file names and your domain name. As they are so important to your search engine strategy, some research on your part is going to be necessary to make your stable of keywords as powerful as possible.

## *Audience Research*

How you conduct your audience research depends a lot on your specific kind of business and the resources that you have to hand. For the most part, all you will need is basic marketing knowledge of your current client base and a likely percentage of how many of them are on the web. This knowledge will also help you gauge how to best word your site copy and sell your products once these web users arrive at your site.

The basic knowledge you need would cover would include:

- Age group
- Gender
- Culture
- Education level

A quick client survey will probably give you most of these answers. A question within the survey asking if they have an email address (and what that email address is), will also give you a fair idea of the percentage that use the Internet to find what they want.

## Keyword Research

Next, you will need to familiarise yourself with what the majority of web users are looking for. There are a number of different sites and tools that can help you do this, but be warned that a lot of these services are uncensored, and you may see some quite unsavoury search queries along the way.

### 'Top 100' Lists

www.searchwords.com
www.searchterms.com
http://50.lycos.com/

There are quite a few sites on the web that provide a list of the top 100 search words used in the major search engines. Some will even let you click through to the search results for a chosen word or term to see who ranks as 'top dog' for this query. Such sites are a good starting point, but the results are nearly always a month old, and not as revealing as a voyeur can be.

### Search Voyeurs

www.webcrawler.com/voyeur_wc
www.excite.com/voyeur_xt

These handy tools are featuring on an increasing number of sites and search engines, but so far the closely related Excite and Webcrawler are doing it best. When you visit the page, a live 'ticker' will appear, showing you a sample of exactly what people are searching for at that moment. Again, you can click on any word or query to see what the top results are, but the most educational thing about a voyeur is the insight it gives you into web users and how they search. You will notice a lot of search queries in the form of a question ('how do i get rich quick?') and many more as a mere collection of words (get rich quick ideas). You will also notice that some search purely in lower case (apples in california united states), while others use upper case letters where they think it appropriate (apples in Texas United States).

Finally, the most revealing thing about a voyeur is how often misspellings feature in search queries. It really is something you have to see to believe, and is so prevalent that it will actually comprise part of your keyword strategy.

### Live Words and Phrases
**www.analogx.com/contents/download/network/keyword.htm**
**www.analogx.com/contents/online.htm**

As yet, there is no site that will let you see a list of the top search words and phrases right now, but there is some software that will let you do it. It's for PC only, but it's free - and very enlightening. Those that cannot use the software (and even those that can) will benefit greatly from the weekly posting of the top results across the last seven days at the support site for the software.

It's called Keyword Live, and it shows you the top 100 keywords and phrases being used in several popular search engines in real time. The words and phrases are shown in separate windows, and you can actually watch the popularity of search queries rise and fall as it happens.

With this, you can watch a particular keyword or phrase that, while it may only hold top spot for a day, manages to knock such perennials as 'sex' and mp3' off their perch. A good example would be 'card for mum', 'mothers day' and 'mothers day gift ideas' throughout - you guessed it - Mother's Day.

Even more amazing, you can actually watch the reaction to a major news story or advertisement right in front of your eyes as millions of web users search the Internet for more information on what they have just seen, read or heard through other media.

Again, it's something you really have to see to believe, and will go a long way to helping you understand how web users in general think when they are looking for something. You will also, however, have to balance this with knowledge of your target audience.

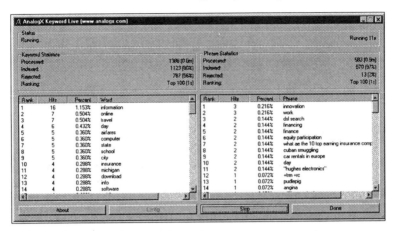

## *Researching Other 'Top' Results*

Use a few likely queries to try and find a business or resource like yours in some of the major 'META Tag reliant' search engines (like Alta Vista and Infoseek). Go and visit the sites that scored a top ten result and have a close look at their page content - and how they have arranged their META Tags.

You don't want to steal these outright (though many people do), rather you want to take a close look at them to get a few ideas and see how you could do better.

## *Drafting Your Keywords and Phrases*

Start with the words that most accurately sum up your business, service and/or product. A great site that will help you come up with some winning phrases based on these is available through the GoTo search engine.

http://inventory.go2.com/inventory/Search_Suggestion.jhtml

By entering a keyword or two at this site, you can immediately see the top phrases used relating to the keyword(s), and how many people made such a search. These statistics are provided by a monthly review of what web users were actually searching for through GoTo over the previous month, and are a pretty good guide to get you started. To give you an example, these were the top results for 'internet marketing' (the figures on the left show the number of queries made using this phrase over the last month):

2975    internet marketing
191    marketing on the internet
161    internet marketing consultant
145    internet marketing strategy

Having previously only suspected that 'internet marketing' was a likely search query for something akin to this book, we now know that it is the most likely, and have a few extra combinations besides.

Using this site to look up the top three or four words that best describe your business will give you a great starting list. It may even present a word or two describing your business or product that you never considered before.

## Synonyms & Related Words

A web user searching for an 'expert in family law' may not use this phrase to find what they are looking for. They could very well look for 'divorce lawyer' or even 'I want half of everything' if you believe what you see in the movies.

## One Word, Many Uses

For some search engines it's a good idea to make words plural or longer wherever possible (markets, marketing, marketed etc.) as they will recognise the shorter word 'market' within these words, and also register a result when someone searches for the longer or plural versions.

## The Layman's View

A web user looking for your business or product may not be as familiar with the related terms as you are. You should be aware of this and include a few terms for the 'layman'. This will require some lateral thought and a few educated guesses, but will help you reach an audience that you might otherwise have missed out on.

## Misspelling Counts

You should also include a few misspellings in your keywords.

- If a vital word is particularly hard to spell, then a few 'phonetic' variations might be of help - this goes especially if your target market is younger or less educated ('phonetic' and 'fenetic' is a good example).

- If a keyword relating to your business is particularly confusing or can be spelled a number of ways, then include the most likely variations ('copywriting' and 'copyrighting' are constantly being confused with each other).

- If there are spelling variations from country to country on an important keyword, then you should include both versions ('gaol' and 'jail').

- Most misspellings, however, will be typos made in haste. The easiest way to find likely 'typos' from your most important keywords is to type them a few times as fast as you can.

## Locale

You should also include a word or two to denote what country and area your business is based in (such as 'uk, London'). Most web users, despite having the world at their fingertips, often search for more local sites and will include such keywords in their search query.

What you should end up with is a series of 50 or so powerful keywords or phrases, ranked according to their importance, for you to choose from when drafting your META Tags, special entry pages and directory submissions.

 *Note - Repeating the same keyword in your META Tags more than three to five times is unlikely to benefit you, and can get you penalised through some search engines. Use the most likely combinations only, then move on to related words and misspellings.*

*Chapter 11*

# Submitting Your Site to Search Engines

### *Are you ready? No, really - are you ready?*

While a submission to a search engine can often take four to six weeks to be listed, the robot that harvests your information may very well visit your page within a few hours or days depending on the submission load and schedule of that search engine. If the page you have listed has any errors on it (or in the META Tags) then you could very well 'trip up' the robot and delay a successful listing.

Check the configuration of any page you are going to submit (your index page and any specially tailored entry pages) to make sure that they are completely functional first. Check and recheck your META Tags to make sure everything is in order.

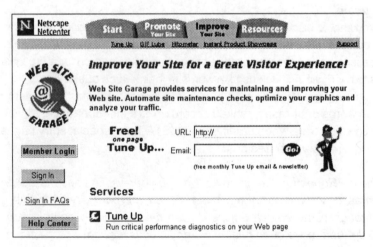

A quick visit to the 'Web Site Garage' at **www.websitegarage.com** should detect any fatal errors. This site lets you enter the URL of a live web page, and will scan it for any bugs or download problems. As this service involves a robot checking your page it is a perfect 'dress rehearsal' for the search engine robots. It also gives you some important 'quality control' information that you should probably address before submitting the site to a directory (see Chapters 4 and 12).

## Multiple Submission of Your 'Index'

There are many sites available on the web that will let you submit to a number of search engines at once. Many of these are 'free', but they aren't always easy to use and there's nearly always a catch (like requiring that you put a banner or link on your site).

The Search Engine Garage at **www.searchenginegarage.com** is refreshingly different in that it will allow you to submit your site to the top 30 search engines with no strings attached. And, while it may not look simple, you will find it far easier to use than any other service on offer. Once you have made your first submission the site automatically fills in the details you need for additional search engines, so for the most part you just have to press 'Go' for each one

in turn. As you do this, it then lets you see the confirmation of each submission in the main window, making it much more informative and reliable than some of the 'set and forget' services on offer.

## Submission of 'Tailored' Entry Pages

As there are only likely to be less than a dozen, it pays to make these submissions separately to each of the targeted search engines. Some search engines like Alta Vista also allow only one submission per day from a single domain, so it's best to leave a 24 hour gap between submitting your 'index' URL and that of your tailored page.

Go to each search engine in turn and look for the 'Submit URL' link. This nearly always appears on the main page. A form will appear asking for the URL and possibly an email address so they can confirm the submission. Refer to your file name list as you do this to ensure that you are entering the correct URL for that search engine. A page that is tailored to the foibles of one search engine could very well violate the 'keyword spamming' rules of another, so all care must be taken lest you be blacklisted for a simple mistake.

| | |
|---|---|
| about.htm | Alta Vista |
| aboutus.htm | Excite |
| keyword.htm | HotBot |
| aboutsite.htm | Infoseek |
| about_site.htm | Lycos |

Above is the example list of file names matched to their corresponding targeted search engine from Chapter 3. Below are the URLs that would be needed for each search engine submission if these files were hosted at 'www.domain.com':

| | |
|---|---|
| Alta Vista - | www.domain.com/about.htm |
| Excite - | www.domain.com/aboutus.htm |
| HotBot - | www.domain.com/keyword.htm |
| Infoseek - | www.domain.com/aboutsite.htm |
| Lycos - | www.domain.com/about_site.htm |

The time it takes for search engines to list your site can vary, but the average times provided below are a pretty good guide:

| | |
|---|---|
| AltaVista: | 1-2 weeks |
| Excite: | 3 weeks |
| Hotbot: | 3-8 weeks |
| InfoSeek: | 6 weeks |
| Lycos: | 2 weeks |

Once your pages are listed - especially your tailored pages - you might want to give them a test run and see how well they perform for a few different search queries.

If you have not scored a top ten result for one of your target queries, then take a close look at the pages that have ranked above you and try to see why they have ranked higher. You may choose to alter your META Tags accordingly and re-submit the page - but do not do so until at least 30 days after your initial submission, or you might be penalised for spamming the search engine.

If you do score that magic top ten result, you should not become complacent. Every day you are on the top ten, someone out there is taking a close look at your META Tag configuration, and may well choose to copy it outright. This is very annoying when it happens, but unfortunately you have very little control over such things unless they use your brand or trademark in their keywords. The best way to deal with such rough play is to quietly accept it as part of life. Imitation is the sincerest form of flattery, after all.

Besides, it pays to occasionally alter your META Tags according to your tracking data (see Chapter 15) and repeat the submission every couple of months. The copycats do not have access to this data, so will forever be playing catch up. Having already proved that they aren't even smart enough to come up with their own keywords, it's a fair bet that they have no overall marketing strategy, so rest assured that the damage from such plagiarism is minimal in the larger sense.

## *Submitting to the Categories*

Most major 'hybrid' search engines now get their category data from the Open Directory Project (see next Chapter), so a successful listing here will automatically get you into these other categories after a space of a few weeks.

Those that run their own category section will invariably have an editorial staff that is very, very, busy - but it often pays to investigate these sections to see if you rate a listing or review. If you do, it will boost your results considerably.

You will have to check the submission guidelines for each of these but, by and large, the rules will be very much the same as those for dedicated directories.

*Chapter 12*

# Submitting Your Site to Directories

**You will need to go beyond a simple page check before you submit it to a directory (though if it takes too long to download, or is incompatible with the browser that the submission editor uses, then it is unlikely to be listed favourably).**

Remember that in this case it is going to be reviewed by a real person, so what is on offer and how it is presented is going to be looked at with a much more discerning eye - often by someone who is very knowledgeable of your kind of business. (Obviously if they are editor of the category where your business should be listed, then they have some level of interest or expertise in this area.)

If the editor arrives to see a site that is disorganised, 'under construction' or misleading in any way, then the submission will be rejected outright.

You not only have to have your site ready, but all of the elements required for your submission such as page title and site description (these have to be entered manually into an online form). It really pays to sit down and compose these elements offline, rather than try to type them 'live' at the submission page.

This way you have ample time to experiment with adding those all-important keywords while keeping the description as objective (and descriptive) as possible.

## *Submitting to 'Yahoo!'*

Yahoo! is the hardest directory to get listed in, but the most worthwhile due to its ongoing popularity and the subsequent boost you get in 'link sensitive' search engines. It is also the directory that will require the most preparation on your part, as the page title and description you provide is more likely to be altered if it is not 'up to scratch' and the edited listing that results is almost impossible to change.

## Create a Draft Document

You will need to create a draft document in your standard word processing program in which to keep the elements of your submission. This will let you collect and arrange these components at your leisure, and also allow you to resubmit your site quickly and easily at a later date (should your submission 'fall by the wayside').

Start by going to Yahoo! and finding the category that is most relevant to your site. (If there are any additional categories in which you think you should be listed, then 'cut and paste' these into your draft submission document - see below.)

You greatly increase your chances of getting listed if you choose the most appropriate category for your submission. Choosing a 'regional' category also increases your chances of getting listed. Also, despite all of your hard work in creating a resource, your site will still be classified as a commercial one and should be listed under a category within 'Business_and_Economy'.

Finding the right category is pretty straightforward. Just pretend you are a customer looking for your business through Yahoo! (use one or two of your top keyword or phrases) and check out the categories that it suggests. Look at the other sites listed in these categories and pick the one that is most relevant to you. If a competitor or two is listed in that category, then it's a fair bet that you belong there too. If the category looks crowded, try and dig a little deeper (again, 'regional' sub-categories are a good bet).

Take a very close look at the other sites listed in the category you wish to use for your submission and how they relate to the descriptions allowed by the editor. This should give you a good sense of their editorial 'style' and what length of description you are likely to get away with. Make a note of the average description length and set this as your maximum when drafting.

Also take a close look at the page titles that are listed in the category and see if they correspond with the actual page title of the page it links to. Some editors are more exacting about this than others, preferring to stick with the actual page title rather than the one suggested for listing (or a vastly shortened version of either). Once you have a good sense of how the category editor conducts their business, you are ready to start drafting your submission to them.

## *Drafting Your Submission*

Yahoo! requests the following information for any category submission:

- Title
- URL
- Description
- Categories
- Contact Info
- Final Comments

### Title

You should make sure that your most vital keyword appears in the page title, and that the page title you are providing for the submission corresponds with that of the page you are submitting.

Try to stick with the average page title length for that category and do not include any promotional text (like 'best deal or 'great site'). You may also notice that the listings in each category are alphabetical, but trying to capitalise on this by giving a 'AAA Business' page title is not advisable. Stunts like this not only force the editor to alter the page title, (meaning vital keywords could go as well) but can more likely than not see your submission being rejected immediately.

### URL

Yahoo! frowns on entries that submit anything other than the 'default' or 'index' page. If you have a valid reason for doing otherwise, then you should justify this clearly in the 'Final Comments'.

It should also be noted that Yahoo! give preference to sites hosted at their own domain. Another reason to consider taking this step.

## Description

Officially, you are allowed around 25 words, but remember that the closer you are to the average listing in the category, the less likely it is that the editor will trim it. Usually 12-15 words is the norm.

Be as objective as possible, while using as many keywords as you can. This takes some effort, but is worth doing right. If an editor suspects that you are weighing the description with keywords, he will chop the offending terms mercilessly. An overly hyped description is more likely than not going to get your submission rejected outright - and even if it does make it through, the editor will rewrite the description given in its entirety.

## Categories

Simply submitting to the wrong category is enough to get a submission rejected. An editor is not going to refer it to a more fitting category on your behalf. However, if you submit to the most fitting category and the listing is accepted, then a listing in the additional categories that you suggest here will be considered. Only suggest another category if you truly think it belongs, and do not suggest more than two.

## Contact Info

Here you provide your full name and email address. You will also need to provide your company name, phone number, fax, address, city, state/province, postcode and country. Including these details in your draft submission document not only makes it easier to 'cut and paste' the details into the submission form, but also lets you check these details carefully to make sure that they are all correct.

## Final Comments

Use this for any comments as mentioned above, plus a short sentence on the purpose and value of your site (what it contains, who it is intended for etc.). You might also want to include a brief and polite 'thank you for considering our site' message. It may not help, but it certainly can't hurt.

## Making Your Submission

Once you've gathered all of your information and checked it for accuracy, go to your chosen submission category at Yahoo! and click on 'suggest a site' while you are in that category. From here it's a simple matter of following the step-by-step submission process, and cutting and pasting the information from your draft submission document into the relevant boxes.

## Chase Up Your Submission

If you are not listed within a few weeks, repeat the submission. As we've pointed out before, Yahoo! editors are very busy and may have overlooked your site. You can re-submit every couple of weeks if you wish, as there is no official penalty for doing so - but often it can take up to 8-10 weeks or more for Yahoo! to finally get around to you.

If, after all this, you still fail to get listed, perhaps you need to take a closer look at your site and ask yourself if it is of sufficient quality (take a look at other sites that have made it, to get an idea of what the editor deems 'acceptable'). Yahoo! does have an appeals process, but it is even longer and more drawn out than that of submissions. If you do wish to appeal, contact them with your concerns and explain why you think your site is of sufficient quality for listing and what it has to offer to the category in question. Don't do this by email, rather send a fax or letter by 'snail mail' to their head office.

Such measures should not be necessary if yours is a quality site that belongs in your chosen category, and you play by the rules as outlined above.

## About Yahoo!'s 'Business Express' Program

Yahoo! do offer a program that ensures your site will be considered within 7 working days, but this involves a hefty processing fee and does not guarantee that your submission will be successful.

## *Submitting to the 'Open Directory Project'*

A successful submission is much easier to achieve at the Open Directory project, as they have so many editors. However, these editors are volunteers, and submitting a site to the ODP does present a few problems of its own.

The submission process is very much like that of Yahoo! and the similar rules apply. You will need to find the category which best suits your site, then click 'Add URL' while in this category.

You will be presented with a form asking for:

- Title
- URL
- Description
- Contact Email Address (optional)

As with Yahoo!, it is advisable to do some research in your chosen category to get an idea of the quality and type of sites already listed and the editing style. It is likely that there will be more than one editor of your category, making this a little harder to judge.

If you follow the same rules of play as for Yahoo!, then you should find your carefully worded title and description listed almost word for word in anything from two hours to two weeks.

## *Tip*

If you wish, you can also use your site's tracking facilities to see if and when your submission has been considered. When your logs reveal a visit by 'add.Yahoo.com', this indicates that your URL has been validated by the system. A referral from 'http://surf.Yahoo.com/submissions/' shows that a Yahoo! editor has visited your site as a result of your submission (see Chapter 15 for more details on tracking and the difference between a 'visit' and a 'referral'). If you aren't listed a few weeks after such a visit, then you have most probably been rejected.

## Are You Already Listed?

As a lot of OPD editors are real 'go-getters', you may very well find your site listed already; check first before you end up needlessly re-submitting your site. If you do find yourself listed and wish to make alterations to the description, then contact the editor(s) of the category in which it is listed with your politely worded requests for alteration. There is an email facility available through the site, and you should use it for such requests (not re-submit the site to that category).

If there is a category that you think is more fitting than the one you are already listed in, then by all means submit your site to that category, but it's usually a good idea to make sure that the alterations to the existing entry are made first. Why? Because the online system that the editors use to accept submissions allows them to 'import' any existing reviews of a submitted site with a click of a button. Many editors use this option if it is available, as it saves time and makes for a more consistent directory.

## Is Your Listing Correct?

As you would imagine with a volunteer workforce, quality control can suffer from time to time. If you find that your listing includes a major grammatical or spelling error, then drop the editor(s) a line about it immediately, before the entry is listed 'as is' in AltaVista, HotBot, Google or Lycos as part of their regular category harvest. If the faulty entry happens to be live when one of these search engines drops by for its regular update, then it will remain in their category sections, complete with error, for weeks or even months before they return to harvest the updated version.

Not all web users know how such things work, so a glaring error in your site description is most likely to reflect badly on you, not the editor at fault. Be polite about such things, but do not dawdle and get any errors corrected as soon as possible.

## Are You Being Listed Fairly?

There has been a lot of discussion about the intentions of some volunteer editors. While stringent controls are in place to ward off abuse of the system, you could very well find that one of your competitors is the editor of the category in which you wish to be listed. Indeed, what better way to ensure that your page title and description are exactly as you wish them to be?

While it isn't against the rules to list your own site in a category that you edit, exercising unfair editorial controls to give your site an advantage most certainly is. The cardinal sin here is marking your own site as a 'cool site', thus giving it top billing. If you suspect that such things are going on, then you should report the editor in question to the senior editor of that category. If your claims can be substantiated, then justice will be swift.

Despite these shortcomings, a successful and effective listing in the Open Directory project is much easier to achieve than in Yahoo! - and the benefits can be almost immediate.

## Submitting to 'Ask Jeeves'

Your submission to 'Ask Jeeves' is one that you have much less control over. It mostly involves you sending them an email with the URL of your site and a brief description.

Here the site not only has to stand on its own merits, but also be directly relevant to one of the questions currently in the Ask Jeeves database. To find out if such a question (or one close to it) exists, simply go to Aks Jeeves and present the directory with a question that you would expect to relate to your site.

If you find a suitable existing question that lists sites akin to yours, then refer to this question and how your site compares to those currently listed in your email submission.

*Chapter 13*

# Other Submissions and Listings

There are thousands of search engines and directories available to the web user, but you won't have to list in all of them. Rather, you should do a little research and find ones that apply most to your web site.

The best place to start for this kind of research is the 'search engine for search engines' at **www.finderseeker.com** - where you can quickly and easily find search engines and directories by topic and/or region.

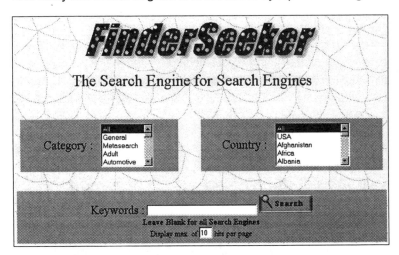

## *Regional Search Engines and Directories*

There should be one or two search engines that specialise in your particular region or locale. This goes especially for sites that have included region-specific information as their 'bait' resource (remember the real-estate agent with the local information?).

Even if you plan on doing business world wide, you should still submit your site to local directories, as getting listed in them is easy and every link to your site helps. Also, many web users search for local businesses out of pure habit.

## Speciality Search Engines and Directories

If there is a search engine or directory that is specific to your business or the type of resource(s) you have on offer, then you should definitely submit your site to them. Many web users prefer to find business or resource sites in this way, as they can browse through sites that meet their specific need quickly and easily.

If a directory does not exist for your kind of business or resource, then this is a potential resource in itself. Providing such a directory would make your site the first stop for many web users interested in what you have to offer.

## 'Cool' Sites

These range from directories offering links to the 'best of the best', to formal awards sites that will include a review of your page with the listing. The awards themselves you can probably do without (see 'Awards' in Chapter 14), but getting a positive review in such a directory can mean a lot of traffic.

In addition, there are mailing lists which announce new sites that are of excellent quality. Submitting your site to these can also mean greatly increased traffic. But be warned that most web users who visit your site through such a recommendation would be doing so at the same time, if not within the same day. This kind of 'flash crowd' can overload your server, so make sure it has sufficient bandwidth.

Sites get listed as 'cool' sites only if they offer something truly unique, and/or are of excellent design. Be realistic about how worthy your site is, and if your site is not of a level to rank with the very top 'cool' sites or listings, then don't bother submitting to lesser ones. These smaller sites are nearly always a waste of time and rarely result in enough traffic to make your efforts worthwhile.

## Should You Pay for a Search Engine or Directory Listing?

### No!

If a search engine, directory or other site requires payment before they list you, look elsewhere. Even large search engines that charge a fee for listing are not worth your time, especially when there are so many 'free' search engines that are far more popular with web users.

'Goto' is just such a search engine, but tries to make payment for listing more attractive by suggesting that you 'bid' for nominated keywords on a 'per-click' basis. The higher your bid, the more likely you will get top result for a search query using these words.

A clever model, but again it pays to think about it from the web user's point of view. Would you be more interested in a site that paid to get your attention, or one that appears more relevant to your search query and/or has been recommended independently? Stick with the standard search engines and directories, as sites that ask for money are rarely popular enough to warrant such an expense.

*Chapter 14*

# Encouraging Links to Your Site

**Every link to your site is a potential boost to traffic, so it is in your interest to encourage as many links as possible. Not only will some visitors find your site via such a link, but an increasing number of search engines are using link popularity as part of their ranking procedure. (Of course, the page that links to you will have to be registered with the search engine in question for the link to count in your favour.)**

## *Reciprocal Links*

Asking for a 'reciprocal' link is one of the easiest and most informal methods of boosting your link popularity. It simply involves you finding sites that are closely related to your type of business or the resource(s) you are providing and creating links to those sites on your 'links' page.

You then email those you have linked to, letting them know where their page has been linked to and why ("I thought my customers might find your site useful, so included a link to at www.domain.com/links.htm" or something similar). A polite request for a link to you on their site in return is nearly always honoured in such cases, but it pays to be subtle. You should also include the main URL of your page in such an email so it is clear where it is that you wish them to link to. Ideally you want them to link to your main 'index' page, as this is the one registered with all of the search engines. ("If you think my site at www.domain.com/index.htm would be equally useful to your customers/visitors, then perhaps you would consider a reciprocal link - many thanks etc.")

Keep in mind that large sites such as **www.disney.com** are unlikely to reciprocate such a link, so try to focus on sites of a similar level to yours. You should also keep your 'links' page as tidy, organised and useful as possible to leave those that you have linked to in no doubt as to the value of the link. If they see their site listed under a carefully organised category, (possibly even with a short description or review) they will be much more impressed than if you simply include them in a long list of seemingly anonymous links.

Also, as the site that links to you has to be registered with the relevant search engines for it to be of any real value, you will have to check that it is listed in these. If it isn't, you might wish to reply to their confirmation of a link to you with something like; "Thanks very much for the link. By the way, I noticed that your site isn't listed in 'Google', would you like me to look after this next time I am there?" Alternatively you can just submit them without asking, but it always pay to be polite about such things and it's a nice way to say 'thank you'.

## Link Exchange Programs
There are a large number of 'themed' and random link exchange programs, but they are almost always of more benefit to those running the program than the participants, and give you very little control over who links to you and who you have to link to in return. This is not a good move for a professional web site.

## Web Rings
'Web Rings' are programs that encourage sites of a like nature to include a navigation tool on their page(s), that lets visitors to that site visit other sites on the same subject. Again, this mainly benefits the initiator of the program and can make your site look less than professional.

## Awards
Getting an award from a major site such as Lycos is cause for celebration and you should definitely display such an award on your site with pride, but having a bunch of dopey 'second string'

## Elements of a Successful Awards Scheme

**As there are so many other awards schemes out there already, you should try to come up with an award that is unique in theme. Ideally this theme should be of interest to potential customers and/or related to your business type or chosen 'bait' resource(s).**

Once you have a unique basis for your awards, you will need to set clear and professional criteria for those who wish to apply for one. This should be outlined on a special web page for your awards, making it very clear who should apply for one and how they should do this. To make their submission (and your life) easier, this usually best done with an online form. This way, the information you get is presented in an ordered manner and is much easier to keep up with.

You should also grade your awards (e.g. gold, silver and bronze). This allows you to give awards to (and get links from) a higher number of sites without compromising the integrity of your award scheme.

Recipients of the award should be listed on a special 'winners' page (not your links page). Doing a short review can increase the popularity of your award, but does make it very hard work. It's usually best just to group the winners under 'gold', 'silver' or 'bronze'. If your 'winners' page starts getting crowded, you can break them up into categories very much like a directory would do.

The graphic(s) you present as the award(s) should not only be attractive, but also of a very small file size (no more than two or three kilobytes). They should also be GIFs so you can assign a transparent background, making them compatible with any site's background colour scheme.

Of course when you grant the award, you will need to present it in a way that ensures the recipient puts it on their site complete with a link to you. The best way to do this is by emailing them special HTML code that they can paste into their page that calls up the graphic from your server and displays it on their page. Of course, because you are writing the code, you get to make sure that it links to your 'index' page (not the 'awards' or 'winners' page) and can assign a strong message as the 'ALT text' for the graphic. This isn't as difficult as it sounds, and lets you update the graphic for the award at a future date without having to track down everybody you have given an award to.

Once your awards scheme is set up, you will need to submit it to an awards directory or two. The very best of such directories is the Focus site at **www.awardsites.com**. This, the best and most popular of the awards directories, grades listed awards schemes according to how worthwhile they are. The higher your rating, the more award submissions you will get. There's more information on the site, but if you follow the guidelines above you should score a pretty high rating.

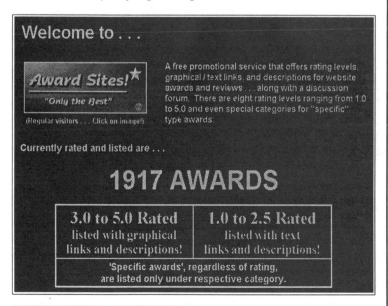

Welcome to . . .

**Award Sites!** ★
*"Only the Best"*
(Regular visitors . . . Click on image!)

A free promotional service that offers rating levels, graphical / text links, and descriptions for website awards and reviews . . . along with a discussion forum. There are eight rating levels ranging from 1.0 to 5.0 and even special categories for "specific" type awards.

Currently rated and listed are . . .

# 1917 AWARDS

| 3.0 to 5.0 Rated | 1.0 to 2.5 Rated |
| --- | --- |
| listed with graphical links and descriptions! | listed with text links and descriptions! |
| 'Specific awards', regardless of rating, are listed only under respective category. | |

awards on your site impresses nobody. Including such awards on your site not only makes you look like a rank amateur, but also slows your download time considerably (each award being a linked graphic you could well do without).

However, running your own awards scheme can definitely pay off, as there are millions of amateur page builders and 'award junkies' out there who just love the recognition. If you do wish to run your own awards scheme, then you will need to do it right to get enough traffic to make it worthwhile. Having a popular awards scheme will mean you reviewing anywhere from 5 to 15 sites a week or more, and you will have to keep up with this religiously.

Again, those who do link to you via the award will have to be registered with the relevant databases for this link to count towards your ranking.

As you might be able to tell, an awards scheme works very much like a reciprocal link arrangement. The main differences being that it brings them to you and is viral in nature (many will find your site after seeing an award and will come wanting one of their own).

## Tracking Links to Your Site

Not everybody who links to you is going to notify you of the link, so occasionally you will have to do a 'spot check' to gauge your link popularity.

The most important search engine to do this through is Google, as link popularity counts for so much here. There is a quick and easy way to see which sites in the Google database are linking to you - you just do a 'link' search using your main URL.

"link:http://wsww.yourdomain.index.htm"

Doing this will bring up a set of results showing which pages currently listed at Google link to your 'index' page. You will notice that this search also shows pages within your own site that link back to the 'index' page, but don't think that these boost your rating, as links from the same domain are discounted in the ranking algorithm.

This neat trick works in just about all the major search engines except Alta Vista, which has its own 'link popularity' function. The best way to enact this is to go to **www.spyonit.com** and choose the 'link alert' function from their 'Swiss Army Spies'. This not only generates a report about who already links to you in Alta Vista, but can also send an email alert when a new link is registered within the database. Spyonit can do so much more, but you'll discover that in the next chapter.

*Chapter 15*

# Tracking Your Results

**An important part of marketing is research. With the right tracking tools, you can not only keep an eye on which initiatives are working (and which aren't), but also find out how the web community in general is responding to your site and even what your competitors are up to.**

## *Tracking Your Site Results*

Wouldn't it be nice to know exactly who is coming to your site and how they got there? Armed with this sort of information, you would be better able to judge your future marketing strategy.

While most web servers offer basic counting services and 'log files', you will need much more information than this to get to know your web site audience - but getting such results need not involve a lot of technical knowledge or expensive software.

The SuperStats service available through **www.mycomputer.com** is ideal for the online marketer. This is a powerful and easy to use 'third party' tracking service that can be used on just about any web site. All you have to do is to join the service and paste the code you are given into the page you wish to track. You can then view your tracking results through the site anytime you choose.

There are three levels of service for this - 'Lite', 'Banner' and 'Professional', but even the free 'Lite' service provides rich and easy to understand information about your visitors. (The 'Professional' service does cost money, but is excellent value. Plus, you can get just as much information from the 'banner' service which, as the name suggests, requires that you put a banner on the page you are tracking in return for the enhanced service. This is one of the few services that make having a banner on your site worthwhile.)

Just some of the information you can track through this service includes:

- **Traffic Reports -**
Including the number of visitors to your site by the hour, day or month and which page(s) they visited while they were there.

- **Visitor Profile Reports -**
Tells you more about the configuration of your visitors' computers and even which browser they use. This information helps you to optimise your site for the majority of your audience. You can also find out when those who speak a different language visit your site. If it turns out that you are very popular in a foreign country, perhaps you should consider a translated version of your page to cater to this audience.

- **Marketing Reports -**
By far the most useful data, this lets you know how your visitors came to arrive at your site. It can tell you if they came from an external link (this is known as a referral) or through a search engine, and even which keywords they used to find your site! You can 'click through' to any of these to find out exactly where the external link is located, or see the results for the search query they made and find out which other sites turned up alongside you. If you watch the search engine percentages closely, you can not only find out which of your listings is most successful, but also when your ranking may be dropping in any given search engine (time to re-submit!) This set of functions also lets you track visits by their individual domain, giving you more data about where your audience is located - and letting you know when a search engine robot has dropped by.

You can watch all of this without your audience being aware of a thing, but if you want to know more about those who visit your site then perhaps it is time to ask.

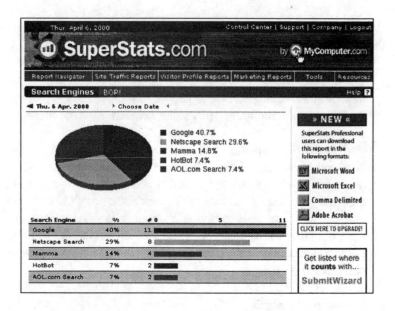

## Visitor Feedback

There are a number of ways to get feedback from visitors to your site, but be aware that the average web user has a very short attention span and is unlikely to want to fill in a complete survey. Also, as most of the web users who arrive at your site do so with a purpose - it is best not to overly distract them from this unless it is to make that all-important sale.

Being aware of this, you may choose to include a simple site poll on your most popular page and update it with one pertinent question per month or week.

There are plenty of 'third party' site polls available on the Internet, even **www.mycomputer.com** offer their own version known as 'EZPoll'. You simply sign up for the free service, configure your poll and paste the code given to you into your web page. This service is easy to set up, and even lets you choose the colour scheme of the site poll. You can also set it to either display the ongoing results or keep them secret, and restrict the number of times each visitor is allowed to vote (i.e. once per day/week or once only).

You can then go to the site and access your results and/or change the questions/options available. What's best about this is you can do it from anywhere and you don't have to re-paste new code into your page each time you make such a change.

Another way to get visitor feedback is to provide a 'Guestbook'. This allows visitors to make comments on the site for all to see and as such has its pros and cons. If you do provide a Guestbook on your site, you will have to watch it closely to ensure that nothing untoward or abusive is posted there.

If you do want to get more information out of your customers, and potential customers, then it is best to do so via a mailing list (see Chapter 17).

## Watching the Web

The best way to stay ahead of the game is to keep a sharp eye on developments that may impact on your business, and there is no easier place to do this than on the Internet. One site in particular can help you track important events as they happen.

## Spyonit.com
### www.spyonit.com

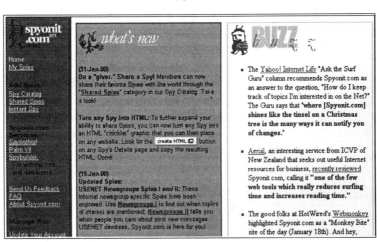

'Spyonit' is a powerful and almost omnipresent tool that constantly scans the web for the latest information. On offer is a choice of 'Spies' that you can configure to tell you when something on the web has changed in a certain way. A lot of people use this to find out when there is a new recipe at Gourmet.com, or when 'Sound of Music' is going to be on television in their area, but the craftier web users make good use of the 'Swiss Army Spies'.

Just to give you an example or five, you can set a 'Swiss Army Spy' to let you know when someone mentions or links to you, or when one of your competitors goes online with their own web site (and after, when they change or update it). Those who worry about such things may also wish to use this 'page change' alert to monitor their own web site - this would let you know immediately if somebody managed to 'hack' into it. A separate 'spy' can also constantly monitor your web site, immediately alerting you if the server is down.

There are even special Usenet spies that you can set to monitor newsgroups and notify you when your business or product is mentioned (see Chapter 18 for more on newsgroups).

**Knowledge is power, use it.**

*Chapter 16*

# Unsolicited Email (Spam)

# DON'T
# DO
# IT

*Chapter 17*

# Targeted Email and Mailing Lists

**While unsolicited email is one of the most widely reviled marketing methods on the Internet (and subsequently hazardous to your business), combining the technology of email with 'permission-based' marketing can generate a lot of positive interest in your web site. The basic principles of permission-based marketing are simple - be polite and invite. By providing the web user with an active choice, you ensure that the marketing messages you send to them are anticipated and relevant to their interests.**

Once you have a growing list of interested parties, you are going to be tempted to email them every time you have something on offer. This is a very bad idea, and sure to annoy those who have trusted you with their email address.

Rather, you should plan for regular mailings and make it clear to those who might wish to join the list how often they can expect an email from you, and in what way(s) it will benefit them.

All of this leans toward the 'opt-in mailing list' model, whereby you provide information about the regular mailings available through you and invite others to join the list. As with your web site, your mailing list needs to offer something of value to the recipient for it to succeed.

Those who join the list could receive or share information via any of the following models:

- **Standard Mailing List -**
  Whereby you send a regular email to the subscribers notifying them of changes to the site, special offers, or anything else that might be of potential interest or value.

- **E-Zine -**
  As with a standard mailing list, but with more content within the email itself, containing articles of interest and full details of any upcoming specials and/or promotions.

- **Discussion List -**
  This model allows subscribers to have discussions by email on a topic that is relevant to your business or service. This requires a lot more work on your part, as you would have to 'moderate' the discussion to keep the list as useful as possible to all concerned.

There are several tools you can use to run and regulate a mailing list. Which one you choose will depend on the type of mailing list you wish to run, the number of subscribers, and the professional image that you wish to project.

## Option 1 - Web-based or Supported

**www.listbot.com**
**www.egroups.com**

There are many such services available that will let you run anything from a standard mailing list to a fully archived discussion list. However, nearly all of these options involve sponsored taglines in the emails you send and banners on the archive sites.

## Option 2 - Your Default Mail Program

The free mail program that came with your web browser has many tools that can help you run a standard mailing list or E-Zine with up to 500 subscribers. The downside here is that you have to work very hard at making sure that those who 'opt-in' are added to the list and, more importantly, those who 'opt-out' are removed immediately.

### Option 3 - Specialised Software

**www.greatcircle.com/majordomo**

Majordomo is by far the most popular software choice for those wishing to run a mailing list. It can not only handle anything from a standard mailing list to a full-blown discussion list, but also automate the 'opt-in' and 'opt-out' functions.

## Promoting Your Mailing List

The best way to get your mailing list growing is to outline the benefits of joining on a special page at your web site and provide a quick and easy 'opt-in' function here. It always helps to include the instructions for 'opting out' directly underneath, so the web user knows that they have that choice.

Emailing unsuspecting web users and inviting them to join your mailing list borders on Spam, but there are exceptions. For instance, if you ran a competition on your web site to gather email addresses of potential customers, you would have to include an option upon submission that lets the visitor choose whether or not they would like to receive further promotional mailings from you. But, if you really wanted to push it, you could send a confirmation email to wish them luck in the competition and include a quick message about the benefits of your mailing list. You would however have to make it very clear that this is the only email they were going to receive as a result of their entry (unless they win, of course!)

If you wish, you can also promote your mailing list via the central database at **www.liszt.com**, where thousands of mailing lists are arranged by category or interest.

## Keeping Strict Standards

Do keep up with your mailing list schedule. If it's weekly, make sure that is goes out at the same time on the same day, so your audience knows when to expect it. Monthly mailings are usually best sent out on the first business day of the month.

Do not contact subscribers outside of the schedule you have set for the mailing list. If you have described the mailing list as 'monthly' but send extra messages to subscribers every other week, then you will find many in your audience tuning out.

If you are providing a function at your site that lets web users subscribe simply by submitting their email address, then you should set up your mailing list so that those who have 'opted-in' in this way must reply from the email address they have provided to confirm the subscription. This stops pranksters and mischief- makers from polluting your list with unwanted addresses.

Keep on top of those 'opt-out' commands. If someone wants to stop receiving mail from the list, then they should be taken off the list immediately. If you wish, you can send a single email confirming the 'opt-out' and thank them for participating, but any other email after this would be a betrayal of their trust and tantamount to Spamming.

If you are running a moderated discussion list, you will have to maintain this regularly, often every day. If a lot of traffic is going through your discussion list, you should also provide subscribers with the option to subscribe to a 'digest' version, letting them see all of the discussions without having to download umpteen emails every day.

## Mailing Lists and Customer Feedback

Running a discussion list provides you with the most sophisticated customer feedback, but if you are after raw data, you may choose to use a mailing or two to find out more about your subscribers. Rather than making this text-based (which is rather clunky and unlikely to get you a good response), you should instead provide a quick introduction to the survey in your email and link to an online version of it at your site.

As mentioned in Chapter 15, it is unlikely that those who have come looking for information on your site will take the time to fill in such a survey. However, a web user who is motivated enough to join your list in the first place will be much more likely to participate. You should also offer those who take part in the survey something of value, such as free entry into a competition or a product discount.

*Chapter 18*

# Newsgroups: The Right Way

Newsgroups, put simply, are topical discussion groups or notice boards based on an individual topic, interest or locale. They allow web users with similar interests to provide and exchange information. You may notice that Usenet newsgroups work very much like 'discussion' mailing lists, in that thsey are used to exchange thoughts and ideas on a particular topic, and can 'subscribe' or 'unsubscribe' from a group at any time.

It is here where the similarities end however, as Usenet newsgroups are more readily available to the general public and are nearly always unmoderated. Also, they are largely unregulated and there are so many of them (over 40,000 at last count) that each one of them comprises a separate 'community' of participants that more or less judge for themselves what is appropriate for discussion and what is not.

This is why it is not only important to know the general rules of posting to Usenet, but also to carefully research any group that you wish to post to - making sure that the message you wish to relay is relevant and welcome.

## *Accessing Usenet Newsgroups*

There are three main ways to access newsgroups:

- **Via Web Servers -**
  The most popular of these is DejaNews at **www.deja.com**, but this method of reading and posting to newsgroups is

slow and fiddly at best. It is however very handy for looking up past messages, as it keeps an almost complete archive of every post to Usenet.

- **Via your Default Mail Program -**
  The free mail program that came with your browser is more than capable of allowing you to read and post to newsgroups. Depending on your ISP, there should be in excess of 30,000 newsgroups available to you immediately and your ISP should be able to provide you with details on how to set this up. Some find the newsreaders in such programs - especially that of Outlook Express - to be less than 'user-friendly', but for the occasional poster it will more than suffice.

- **Via a Specialised Program -**
  Forte Agent is the most popular mail software amongst Usenet aficionados. There is also a free newsreader (Free Agent) available for download via their site at www.forteinc.com. Be aware, however, that while this software does have many 'news-friendly' gadgets, it is not the prettiest interface in the world and can make Usenet more of a chore for those who simply want to read and post.

## Avoiding Common Mistakes

Newsgroups are so many things to so many people that it would be pointless to try and explain the myriad of rules and regulations that exist for each individual group in this single chapter. We can however warn you of the major pitfalls of promoting your business through newsgroups, and stop you from making any mistakes that could very well come back to haunt you.

### Lurk First

You need to find out about your chosen community before you attempt any level of marketing within it. Take care to read the FAQ and/or charter for the newsgroup if one exists, and spend at least a week watching how the community behaves by reading the posts without making any yourself (this is commonly known as 'lurking'). Pay particular attention to how they respond to 'off topic' posts and Spam.

## Don't Spam

One of the most common mistakes most business users make when they first discover newsgroups is to barrel straight in to one that they consider most relevant to their product or service and post a message plugging their site.

While it may seem advantageous to post details regarding your web site to a relevant newsgroup, such commercialism is widely frowned upon and can have dire consequences for your business. Newsgroups are also very much community based, and most that participate in them fervently guard the integrity of their discussion topic(s).

As such, 'Spamming' the group is not only likely to alienate your audience here, but also get you some quite unsavoury responses (that will be archived for all to see) and possibly even some unwanted attention from those in the group who act as 'guardians' against Spam. These are the individuals who will more than likely do everything they can to get your account terminated and/or post your personal details on the Internet.

## Reply at the Bottom

When you do start replying to some messages within the newsgroup, be careful to keep the indented quote of the previous poster at the top of your message and post your reply to it at the bottom. For some bizarre reason, Outlook Express prompts you to post at the top, but as you can imagine this makes following a lengthy discussion quite hard to follow if someone replies to your post in turn.

## Participate!

The best way to promote your site through a newsgroup is to bring something of value to the community (such as your expertise). By doing so in a friendly manner on a regular basis, you stand more chance of getting traffic to your site by providing a link to it in the signature you provide at the bottom of each of your posts (this is commonly known as a 'sig file').

### The 'four line' Sig File Rule

Your signature file should be subtle and no more than four lines long (some newsgroups even have rules in their charter that it should be shorter than this, but four lines is generally treated as an acceptable maximum).

In it you should include your name (or nickname) and a link to your site. A sales message would be too much here, but a short description of the site is usually tolerated. If you have a domain that comprises both - such as **www.buymybook.co.uk** - then all the better.

What you will find by participating intelligently and helpfully is that participants within the group will want to know more about what you do, and follow this link through to your web site.

### Beware of Trolls

There are some that think it's fun or clever to disrupt newsgroup communities by posting controversial, inflammatory or just plain stupid information to get a reaction - and any kind of reaction pleases them. These individuals are known as 'trolls'. Don't respond to trolls, don't berate them - in fact don't even berate others for responding to them.

Once a troll gets the attention he is looking for, he will stick around for more. Some can even turn quite nasty if you attack them, as most have 'anonymous' access to newsgroups and see themselves as being largely invincible. Ignore them, ignore them, ignore them. Soon enough they will go away and find other schoolboys to play with.

## Avoiding Spambots

By posting to newsgroups, you leave yourself open to Spammers. The most common tool Spammers use to garner email addresses from newsgroups are 'Spambots' (these are programs that harvest email addresses from live or archived newsgroup posts). For this reason, you should put a 'spamblock' in your reply email address and never, ever include your email address in the text of any post.

Some determined Spammers will even target one newsgroup in particular and 'harvest' the email addresses of the participants manually (i.e. taking out the Spamblocks) to make up what they see to be 'targeted' lists. Being the loveable rogues that they are, they will then sell these lists to other Spammers. Depending on the newsgroup and how likely it is to be targeted, within a few weeks or months of your first post, you can almost guarantee that your Inbox will be crammed with Spam.

For this reason, it pays to not only include a Spamblock, but also use a 'reply' email address from a disposable web-based email account, rather than your main access account. Many 'Usenetters' do so via YahooMail or Hotmail, but the best of such web-based accounts is available at **www.another.com**. This site not only gives you access to thousands of domain names (letting you come up with an email address that is themed to your business and/or chosen newsgroup), but also allows you up to 20 email addresses on the one account. This means that you can drop an email address once it becomes 'polluted' and pick another almost straight away. There is also a site at www.spammydodger.co.uk that gives full step by step instructions on how to do this effectively and elegantly.

### *Don't Spam Community Members!*
Just as you wouldn't appreciate someone 'harvesting' your email address and sending you unwanted email, those who participate in your chosen community are just as likely to take offence. More so, they will be greatly offended that someone from 'within the circle' has done such a thing. Such an action will almost certainly see you shunned from the group.

Finally, you should be aware that while your chosen newsgroup may very well be a targeted audience, it will not result in more than a few hundred hits to your web site over time, as opposed to the thousands that can result from a successful search engine listing.

Chapter 19

# Marketing in Real Life

**Not all of your marketing efforts need to be online. In fact once you own a functional web site, the ease with which you can market your business increases dramatically! The key to success here is a short and memorable domain name.**

This single line of text not only aids your branding, but also informs those who see it where more information about you can be found.

## From Your Business

### Company Stationary

Make sure that your domain name is printed on everything that goes out of your office. Business cards, letterheads, fax headers, invoices, receipts, envelopes - everything! Your domain name should appear immediately under your logo, or somewhere equally prominent.

### Signage

This not only includes your shop front, but any company vehicles as well. As not all of the people who see your signage will be familiar with your business, you might also wish to present a reason for visiting the web site directly above the domain name. (Examples of this would include "buy your widgets online and save" or "find free tips/advice/recipes/etc. on our web site").

### Brochures/Flyers

Again, there will need to be a specific motivation for those who have received your brochure to visit your web site (i.e. what is available on the web site that isn't in the brochure). Depending on how confident you are about the percentage of potential customers who have Internet access, you may even choose to thin out your brochure or flyer considerably, using it instead to drive recipients straight to your site.

### Merchandise
If you have any company merchandise such as caps, t-shirts, fridge magnets, stickers etc. then you should feature your domain name on these prominently. Pens, mouse mats, desk caddies, document holders and other items that would normally be kept close to the computer are also good for this.

### Products
Any packaged products should also be branded with your domain name - especially if there is more information regarding the product and its usage on your web site.

## In Print Media

### Articles
You may have noticed reluctance by journalists to print your address or phone number in articles resulting from your press releases. Funnily enough most have no objection to printing a domain name, especially if the article is about your site.

### Classifieds
It's quite simple, really - classified ads are mostly charged at a 'per word' rate. Your domain name is one word that, besides being an address, also identifies your business and/or includes a strong sales message. That's good value.

### Display Ads
Display Ads charge according to the amount of space you use. Again, this single line of text can say and do so much that it should be one of the major elements of any print ad.

## 'Yellow Pages'

As so many are now using the Internet, as their primary form of communication, your commercial phone book listing or ad should feature your email address and domain name, as well as your address and phone number.

# Other Media

### Radio

If you've bought radio time before, you may be aware of how hard it is to cram in all those important details about your business into 30 seconds. You will note that a lot of businesses are using radio to drive listeners to their web site these days, but here your domain name needs to be largely phonetic! Also, while some may actually be listening in front of their computers, most will be in the car - so the domain name needs to be short and memorable too.

### Television

Again, a domain name helps you fight that 30-second restriction. If the main purpose is to drive viewers to the site, you may even find that a 15-second commercial suits your needs.

### Charities and Sponsorship

It is no longer 'sponsored by ACME Widgets', but 'sponsored by www.acmewidgets.com'.

## The Sky's the Limit

You domain name is a single word that defines your business and makes you easy to locate; use it everywhere. Mention it in conversation whenever you can, put in on your answering machine... have some bookmarks made up and leave them in library books that relate to your business... print your domain name in large letters on a kite and take your kids to the park for the day...

Communicate this powerful branding tool to the public whenever, wherever and however you can.

# Glossary

**Ad Slot**
Refers to the space on a website where a banner or advert sits.

**Animated GIF**
An image or picture that moves – utilised mainly for banners and advertising but also widely used for enhancement images.

**Bandwidth**
Essentially refers to transfer rates and speed of download through a given medium. The higher the size of a file or image, the more bandwidth is needed to transfer it to a recipient and the slower the upload of a page.

**Banner**
An advert linked to a product or site offering goods or services.

**Bookmark**
A feature allowing your readers to add your site to their favourites list, making their return at a later date simpler.

**Bot**
Usually a programme used to search out information on the Internet but can also refer to any programming code that is designed to perform a specific function.

**CGI programming**
(Common Gateway Interaction) Programming or script (usually PERL) that runs a programme on a web server. For example, forms, page counters and guest books.

**Clickstream**
The name given to the route a visitor takes through a website. By clicking through links and navigating your site a visitor leaves a trail that will show you the most and least popular areas, or the most common exit, thus allowing you to streamline your site to its best effectiveness.

**Click Through**
Usually applies to the number of visitors who click through on an advertising banner, although can equally be applied to other on-site links.

**Cookies**
A cookie stores certain information on your visitor's hard drive, that you have programmed, relating to your site. You can use cookies to track when a customer returns to your site, which pages they visited whilst there or to store passwords for return visits.

**CPM**
Cost per thousand impressions.

**Cybersquatter/cybersquatting**
Someone who tries to pre-empt popular web names and registers them with the intention of selling later at a high price.

**Data Mining**
Utilising any method of data analysis.

**Direct Response**
Usually refers to the click through rate of advertising in the Internet allowing auditors to establish a click-rate and follow a marketing campaign.

**Domain name**
An Internet identification name that specifies where your computer can be contacted. It is written as a series of letters separated by full stops and slashes; for instance ours is net-works.co.uk

**Download**
The process of copying a file from one machine (usually the host) to another (usually yours).

**Dynamic HTML (DHTML)**
The next step up from HTML allowing more control of design and features on a web page.

**Email address**
An address which identifies you on the Internet and allows others to send you Email. There may be many people at a domain name, so the Email address can identify a particular person at a particular address. It is made up from your name, the symbol @ (pronounced at), and the domain name. E.g. *sales@ networks.co.uk.*

**E-zine**
A magazine or trade journal that is transmitted in electronic form, usually email.

**Encryption**
Converts input data, such as credit card details, into a coded format to ensure security during transmission.

**FAQ**
Frequently Asked Questions. This is a document found in most Usenet groups, but can also be a legitimate feature of any website. It will have questions (and answers) that are most commonly asked by customers.

**Firewall**
It will not protect you from flames, but it is a security measure. It prevents access to a LAN from outside networks, e.g. from the Internet. Many companies do not want others to be able to access their LAN.

**Frames**
A way of presenting more than one web page in the same browser window and creating the

impression they are all one page. Each frame can then be scrolled independently of the others.

**FTP**
File Transfer Protocol. The transfer of files from one computer to another, most usually from your computer to your ISP in order that files can be viewed on the Internet.

**GIF**
Graphic Interchange Format. A file format for graphics used on the Web.

**Home page**
It is the first page of a company's web site and the one you will be taken to as a default.

**Host**
Another computer on the Internet which allows users to connect to it. An ISP's computer is a host computer.

**HTML**
Hypertext mark-up language. You need to know this language to create documents to go on the World Wide Web.

**HTTP**
Hypertext Transfer Protocol. The way to transfer HTML documents between the client and the Web server (so others can then see them on the WWW).

**Hypertext**
Text on your computer screen which you click to take you to another document in the same web site or at another. Hypertext links form the basis of the World Wide Web. When creating a web site the author uses HTML to put up hypertext.

**Image Map**
A graphic, that has been 'mapped' with each area linked to a page on the website.

**Impressions**
The number of times a web page has been accessed or visited.

**Intranet**
A network of networks that interconnects within a single organization. The sites within an Intranet are generally closed to the Internet and are accessible only from within the organization.

**IP**
Internet Protocol. This is a standard which devices on the Internet use to communicate with each other. It describes how data gets from its source to its destination.

**IP address**
Your domain name uniquely tells the Internet who you are. Computers need to know this but they prefer to deal in numbers

so your domain name has a decimal notation known as your IP address.

**Java**
A programming language used to create applets.

**Link**
A link that takes your visitors to another part of your site or to another site.

**Listserv**
An computerised mailing list supply system.

**Lurking**
'Listening' to discussions on a newsgroup without posting or contributing.

**Mailing Lists**
Similar to a newsgroup in that they are generally topic specific but carried out with email messages that are sent to all subscribers.

**Meta Tags**
Coding containing information about the content of a Website. Most commonly used by search engines to find sites relating to a search request.

**Newsgroups**
A topic-specific message board accessed by a news server.

**Rich Media**
Refers to advertising or content including, but not limited to, video, audio, flash, interactive menus and forms, generally any non-HTML features.

**Search Engine**
A directory capable of searching through registered websites for requested content.

**Signature**
A message or contact details attached to the end of email content. Over four lines of signature is frowned upon.

**Spam**
Just don't do it. The email equivalent of junk mail, usually involving sending the same message to numbers of Newsgroups or mailing lists. Persistent offenders can be banned by their ISP.

**Traffic**
The term used to describe how many people visit your website.

**Viral Marketing**
Applies to marketing that is 'spread' with minimal effort from consumer to consumer.

# Net-Works Guide to Searching the Internet

Designed to teach Internet users - from novices to veterans - how to locate information on the Internet quickly and easily.

The author uses jargon-free language, combined with many illustrations, to answer such questions as:

❑ Which techniques and Search Engines work best for your specific needs?

❑ What is the real difference between true 'search' sites and on-line directories, and how do you decide which one to use?

❑ How do the world's most powerful Search Engines, such as Yahoo!, Alta Vista, Lycos, Infoseek and Excite, really work?

❑ Are there any 'special tricks' that will help you find what you want, faster? (The answer is YES!)

The book also demystifies complex search techniques involving 'Boolean operators', as well as explaining how to use Meta-Search Search Engines to check several Search Engines at the same time.

Finally the reader will find a bonus chapter covering Intelligent Agents - special high-tech personal search programs that can be installed on your computer to search automatically the Internet on your behalf.

## Understand Shares in a Day   Second Edition

Shows how the share market really works. Inexperienced investors will learn:
● About different types of shares ... ● Why share
prices fluctuate... ● How to read the financial pages
... ● How shares are bought and sold ... ● How risk
can be spread with investment– and unit trusts ... ●
How to build a portfolio of shares ...● The risks and
rewards associated with Penny Shares
Once this groundwork has been covered, the book
explores more complex ideas which will appeal to both
beginners and more experienced investors alike.
£6.95/$11.95

## Investing in Options: For the Private Investor

A hardback book which shows you exactly how to 'gear' your money
to provide more growth. Step-by-step it teaches how you appraise an
options position, looking at the rewards and risks,
and then how to execute a deal.  There are plenty
of examples to show you exactly how its done and
how to trade profitably.
For the experienced options buyer there are
examples of option combinations which can be used
to create almost any desired outcome.  With options
you can make money whichever direction the market
is moving.

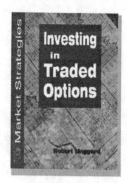

**192 pages**      **£14.95/$27.50**         **Hardback**

## Investing for the Long Term

This book is aimed at those savvy investors who are content to ride
out short term fluctuations in the markets in order
to realise bigger long term gains.  Be it for school
fees, a larger house or retirement, if you need money
in more than 10 years time, this book is for you.
Very comprehensive; covering everything from growth
versus income to understanding company accounts,
and from downturns, corrections & crashes to looking
at the larger economic picture.

**192 pages**      **£14.95/$27.50**         **Hardback**

## Complete Beginner's Guide to the Internet

What exactly is The Internet? Where did it come from and where is it going?

And, more importantly, how can everybody take their place in this new community?

The Complete Beginner's Guide to The Internet tells you: ● What types of resources are available for private, educational and business use ● What software and hardware you need to access them ● How to communicate with others, and ● The rules of the Superhighway, known as 'netiquette'. An indispensable guide to the basics of Cyberspace.

**£5.95/$9.95**

## Smart Guide to Microsoft Office 2000

The Smart Guide to Office 2000 is the first in an exciting new popular

computing series from Net.Works. It is a basic, easy-to-read introduction to the latest Office suite of applications. Filled with short-cuts and tips, this book gives simple directions to help the reader with: ● Creating formatting, and editing professional-looing documents and charts in Word ● Working with formulas, charts, and spreadsheets using Excel ● Communicating with e-mail using Outlook ● Organising your time and tasks using Outlook ● Using the resources of the World Wide Web with Internet Explorer ● Presenting Powerpoint slide shows ● Creating publications, including newsletters, with Publisher, and ● Working with databases to develop reports in Access.

**298 pages    £10.95**

## Complete Beginner's Guide to Windows 98

You can read The Complete Beginner's Guide to Windows 98 on the train,

during your coffee break or while you sit in front of your PC. By the end of each chapter you'll have learned useful skills in Windows 98. By the time you reach the last page you may not get shivers up and down your spine whenever you think of Windows 98, but you'll be using your Windows 98 computer with confidence, working a little bit smarter and having more fun along the way.

**£5.95/$9.95**

# Net-Works Guide to Creating a Website

The World Wide Web has established itself as an important business and communications tool. With hundreds of millions of computer users around the globe now relying on the Web as their primary source of information, entertainment and shopping, it cannot be ignored.

Whether it is to showcase your business and its products, or to present information on your favourite hobby or sport, creating your own Web site is an exciting development. But unless you're familiar with graphics programs and HTML (the "native language" of the Web), as well as how to upload files onto the Internet, creating your Web pages can also be very frustrating! But it doesn't have to be that way.

### Web Publishing Made Easy

This book, written by a Website design and marketing consultant, will help demystify the process of creating and publishing a Web site. In it you will learn:

❏ How to research and plan your site,
❏ What free tools are available that make producing your own Web site child's play (and where to find them),
❏ How to create your own dazzling graphics, using a variety of cheap or free computer graphics programs,
❏ How to put it all together to achieve a great look with a minimum of fuss, and
❏ How to promote your Web site and attract other Internet users to it.

### Advanced Web Design Issues

In addition to canvassing the basics of creating your first Web site, the author also discusses more advanced Web design issues... how to focus your Web site content for your target audience... how to minimise the time taken for your Web site to download... and what lies ahead for the Web and eCommerce... etc., etc.

# Starting and Running a Business on the Internet

Do you want to:
- ✔ Sell your goods all over the world without leaving your office chair?
- ✔ Tap the fastest growing and most affluent market ever?
- ✔ Slash your marketing and advertising costs?
- ✔ Talk to the other side of the world for free?
- ✔ Have access to strategic information only the biggest companies could afford?

*Then your business should be on the Internet!*

Companies are already cutting costs, improving customer support and reaching hitherto untapped markets via the Internet. They have realised the potential for this exciting new commercial arena and they've grabbed the opportunity with both hands. Now you can join in the fun of what is still a 'ground floor' opportunity.

*Starting and Running a Business on The Internet* offers realistic and practical advice for any existing business or budding 'Cyberpreneur'. It also:

- ❏ Helps you get started QUICKLY and CHEAPLY.
- ❏ Tells you which sites 'work', which don't and, more importantly, exactly WHY!
- ❏ Details how to PROMOTE your business online.
- ❏ Shows you how to stay ahead of your competitors.
- ❏ Warns you of the major PITFALLS and shows you how to AVOID them.

# Book Ordering

To order any of these books, please order from our secure website at **www.net-works.co.uk** or complete the form below (or use a plain piece of paper) and send to:

**Europe/Asia**
TTL, PO Box 200, Harrogate HG1 2YR, England (or fax to 01423-526035, or email: sales@net-works.co.uk).

**USA/Canada**
Trafalgar Square, PO Box 257, Howe Hill Road, North Pomfret, Vermont 05053 (or fax to 802-457-1913, call toll free 800-423-4525, or email: tsquare@sover.net)

**Postage and handling charge:**
UK - £1 for first book, and 50p for each additional book
USA - $5 for first book, and $2 for each additional book (all shipments by UPS, please provide street address).
Elsewhere - £3 for first book, and £1.50 for each additional book via surface post (for airmail and courier rates, please fax or email for a price quote)

| Book | Qty | Price |
|---|---|---|
| | | |
| | | |
| | | |
| | | |
| | Postage | |

☐ I enclose a cheque/postal order made payable to 'TTL'  **Total**

☐ Please debit my VISA/AMEX/MASTERCARD/SWITCHs

Number: ☐☐☐☐ ☐☐☐☐ ☐☐☐☐ ☐☐☐☐

Expiry Date: ☐☐☐☐  Signature: _____

Issue No (Switch): ☐☐  Date: _____

Name: _____

Address: _____

_____

Postcode/Zip: _____

Tel/Email: _____

marketbk